This cookbook is the result of Terry Wong's painstaking efforts to recreate his mother's classic recipes from her notes and his palate memories.

These are home-cooked dishes of Singapore and Malaysia – food for family meals and festive feasts from Chinese, Nonya, Malay and Indian cuisines. These days, with fewer families cooking regularly, authentic home recipes along with our food culture are at risk of being lost.

His Mum's classic dishes include Wok-cooked Char Siew, Bean Paste Chilli Crab, Hakka Yong Tau Foo and Pan Mee (Pinched Noodles). Also included are her favourite party dishes like Mee Rebus, Penang Prawn Noodles and Assam Laksa. Traditional favourites such as Steamed Yam Cake, Chai Kuih and Curry Puffs add to the list.

Whether you are just starting out or experienced as a home cook, this cookbook will inspire you. The author enables this with clear, detailed recipes and teaches essential techniques required to master these dishes. And for those new to Malaysian and Singaporean cuisine, this book will enlighten.

As Leslie Tay (ieatishootipost) says: "Terry Wong has decoded the complexity and nuances of Singapore and Malaysian home cooking for the next generation."

Terry uses his God-given talent generously and joyfully to inspire home and community cooking. A paean to his mother's legacy, this book is also an important addition to books about our home food culture.

MUM'S CLASSICS REVIVED

Text copyright © 2016 Terry Wong
Food photography copyright © 2016 Ee Kay Gie

First published November 2016
Reprinted 2018

Photographs on pages 8 and 12 by courtesy of the author,
background on pages 8, 25, 36-37, 51, 70-71, 91, 110-111, 123,
126-127, 153, 159, 176-177, 183, 190-191, 205, 227 and 232-233
courtesy of foltolia.com via Wikimedia, pages 20, 240 and 244
by Kristen Kiong, pages 22, 23, 37, 71, 74 and 126 by the author,
page 95 by Pongsak Deethongngan (123rf.com), and pages 242
and 243 by courtesy of St James' Church.

Published by
Landmark Books Pte Ltd
5001 Beach Road,
02-73/74
Singapore 199588

Landmark Books is an imprint of
Landmark Books Pte Ltd

ISBN 978-981-4189-69-9

Printed in Malaysia

Inspiring Home Cooks

TERRY WONG THE FOOD CANON

MUM'S CLASSICS REVIVED

◦LANDMΔRK◦BOOKS◦

To my Mum, Ung Goay In,
known to many as Auntie Ruby,
for imparting such a wonderful legacy of love,
generosity and passion, not just for cooking,
but for all things in life.

CONTENTS

MISSING MY MOTHER

"She gets up while it is still night;
she provides food for her family..."
~ Proverbs 31:15

Rising before the sun
Walking the markets
Wetting her feet
Seeking out the fresh
Plucking, choosing, haggling
The bagged produce
Straining at her fingers
She made her way home

The taps trickled
The leaves rinsed
The *lesong* rhythmed
The stock bubbled
Ever so softly
For her children were still
In their rooms
in their dreams

The air came to life
Wafting smells
Of pounded herbs
Of tossed sauces

Her children stirred
Scented dreams
Come true

INTRODUCTION

THIS COOKBOOK has been a few years in the planning but many decades in the making. It is an attempt to pass on my mother's recipes to future generations of cooks.

My mother Ung Goay In, or Auntie Ruby as she was affectionately known, was a cook by profession and passion. It was her stepmother – of the *kebaya* generation – who first taught her some amazing Nonya recipes. Her skills were honed further in the multi-cultural environment that West Malaysia was and still is. She did not make significant headway in her profession, certainly not in the same way as we understand culinary career success today. But her cooking was well-loved by many.

Family and friends gathered around my cheerful, bubbly and generous Mum – and if the way into a person's heart is through the stomach, she did that in spadefuls. Her Assam Laksa (page 179), Curry Chicken (page 39), Penang Prawn Noodles (page 173), Hakka Yong Tau Foo (page 143) and Yam Cake (page 207)) were homing beacons.

Unlike many Asian home cooks, she did not have the concept of "secret recipes". She was very generous in sharing her recipes and tips. A humble and constant learner, she connected with other cooks, making them feel like companions on a learning journey rather than competitors.

She was also very adept at making traditional nonya *kuih* and biscuits. Her Kuih Bangket, Kuih Kapik, Peanut Cookies and Pineapple Tarts were extremely popular running up to Chinese New Year. The more orders she received, the more we had to work. They were whole-day affairs. At the end of the day, we looked and smelled like the cookies we made.

My Mum was quite a perfectionist about her cooking. She kept tweaking her recipes till she was satisfied with the results. She often asked for feedback. I recall how disappointed she looked when we told her something was amiss in her dishes. Looking back, I think we could have been more encouraging in our remarks. Sadly, most of us do take our mothers for granted.

When she retired, Mum stayed with us and helped with her grandchildren. We got to enjoy her

MUM AND I WITH WILD-CAUGHT RIVER PRAWNS WHICH
WE MADE INTO HAR LOK FOR CHINESE NEW YEAR, IPOH, 2005

food again. She was then able to cook entirely for pleasure. When my church ran Alpha courses, her dinners were always memorable for guests. Dinners in my home were wonderful as she unleashed her gathered years of experience in every meal. It seemed like she could cook anything, from homey dishes to restaurant fare.

Mum passed away in 2007. We miss her bubbly presence and, of course, we miss her cooking. We miss Mother. We initially tried to improvise with takeaways and home deliveries for daily dinners. However, it came to a point when I knew I had to continue her legacy. I wasn't thinking then of anything more than continuing our family tradition of home-cooked dinners.

The Food Canon Blog

I have always thought that it would be good to help my Mum write and publish a cookbook. When her illness set in, she became incapacitated very quickly. All we could rely on in recreating her dishes was a file of about 30 of her recipes – written down by one of her friends – the rest were just palate memories.

When I put on Facebook a photo of Mum's Wok-cooked Char Siew (page 75) which I made, there were requests for her recipe. That inspired the creation of the food blog. Even then, I was only writing and posting recipes for my friends. I was trying to be silly, to amuse people I was familiar with. Even the title of the blog was tongue-in-cheek. My good friend, Leslie Tay, an established food blogger (ieatishootipost) helped to publicize my blog early on. That drew public attention to it. When I realised that netizens were interested in my Mum's recipes and what I was doing, I knew that I could do my bit to keep some of the traditions of good home cooking alive.

Thus, in an unexpected way, the blog became a memorial to my Mum. Each time I blog about one of her recipes, memories of her are relived.

The blog has also helped me to connect with many who share my interest in the dynamic world of Malaysian and Singaporean cuisine. I have found that those who are studying or living overseas are keen to find authentic recipes and techniques and recreate what their grandmas, mums or aunties have made. It is fascinating how closely intertwined food, family and culture are.

Cuisines and recipes are evolving very rapidly today. Cooking traditions are now better explained through food science. My Mum loved soft-boiled eggs and she would have been very amazed by how perfect soft-boiled eggs can be achieved by *sous vide* appliances. She had no idea that there would be another way to make good Bak Kut Teh. Yet, there still remains an appreciation of the necessity of traditional techniques. The Nasi Lemak rice needs to be steamed. Good Sambal Belacan still needs to be pounded. Claypot Chicken Rice still tastes best cooked in a sand claypot. The wok is still irreplaceable as a simple, yet versatile, appliance.

This Cookbook

Being my first cookbook, it has a strong focus on reviving my Mum's favourite recipes. I have written a helpful article on how you can use these recipes effectively (see page 13).

It is not easy to master a recipe and cook it consistently well. Be patient. I know of some cooks who stop working on a recipe because they "failed" the first time. Keep at it as you will learn from your mistakes. 'Failure' has to do with your expectations. Lower them when you start on a new recipe.

This cookbook needs to be read with other cookbooks and cooking websites in mind. The number of pages could easily be doubled if I included details on regional herbs, spices, vegetables and traditional utensils.

My blog and this cookbook aim to add value to the growing discussion and sharing of dishes and techniques from the Malaysian, Singaporean, Nonya, and other Southeast Asian cuisines, as well as the way they are interacting with other food cultures.

Most of all, I want to inspire the home cook – an endangered species in our hectic, modern world. It is often at the dining table, over a home-cooked meal, that family memories are formed and bonds strengthened. This tradition can easily be lost over the span of a generation, along with time-honoured family recipes.

Likewise, we risk losing our regional, even our country's recipes in a globalized world where the new generation is more enamored by Western celebrity chefs, longing to make Beef Wellington rather than Siew Yoke, mastering a soufflé and ignoring Kuih Kosui.

As a Christian and a pastor, I have also become much more aware of how food and cooking can enrich communities (see page 21). My faith in a Creator whom I know and worship is not restricted to Church services on Sundays. It is something that centers my life and gives meaning to everything I do.

I hope you will find this cookbook enjoyable and useful. Visit my blog and stay in touch. Drop me an email. I will appreciate your feedback.

It is a journey we will take together to keep the recipes we love alive, for the sake of our culture, for the love of home-cooked food, and in memory of those who have cared for us.

Till today, I still miss my Mum very dearly. I am grateful for every gift He has given me through her. I am grateful to God for the legacy she has left behind.

It is my joy to share this with you.

Terry Wong aka The Food Canon
terrywg@gmail.com
foodcanon.com

COOKING FROM MY RECIPES

I HOPE TO GIVE YOU some guidance here on how to make the most of the recipes in this book.

The written recipes my Mum left behind are very brief, with simple lists of ingredients and just a few lines of instructions. As I grew up enjoying these dishes, those brief recipes still proved useful as could I tap on my "palate memories" to work towards the familiar tastes of Mum's cooking. As I do so, I am now able to explain in greater detail how her dishes can be cooked. The recipes in this book are a fruit of that work as I sought to make her recipes more accessible to home cooks.

I wish I could say I that I have recreated every one of Mum's dishes perfectly but that is simply not possible. An interpretation of a recipe is unique to a moment in time and it is difficult to reproduce it exactly. Many factors come into play. The mood of the cook on any given day, the quality of the ingredients, and even the kitchen utensils used can affect the outcome. By reducing the variables through using ingredients from the same source and working with the same utensils to cook them, you can have better control over the result. This is the common practice of restaurants. For the home cook, these variations are acceptable as long as the dish is still delicious and the character of the recipe is retained.

Recipes are helpful as an initial guide but the palate has to take over to fine-tune and approximate the familiar taste. If you have not tasted a dish from a particular recipe before, you will not have the advantage of familiarity. But you can still use your palate to ensure that the flavours are well balanced and delicious.

If you are just a beginner, following the recipes here exactly is a good way to start. Even then, never stop tasting and thinking about what you are doing. For example, the sauces and salt you use may have different degrees of salinity from those I use. For the more experienced cook, you need not punctiliously follow the recipes. You add your own special touch to your dishes, adjusting and adapting recipes according to what comes more naturally to you. A good recipe is often a synergy of other good ones. So, your recipes may interact with mine to result in improved ones.

However good a recipe and your techniques are, you need to start with proper and fresh ingredients. As C.S. Lewis quipped, "No clever rearrangement of a bad egg can make a good omelet." Although our Southeast Asian produce is not seasonal, their quality does change over time. With knowledge of the good produce currently available, you can make adjustments to traditional recipes. Indigenously bred beef used to be tough in days gone by. So, if you are cooking with tender imported beef, you should make adjustments to the recipe and cooking time. In recent years, the quality of our chickens has also improved with the introduction of the French "bare-neck" breed.

Read the essays that teach techniques. Where possible, I have tried to explain why certain ingredients are used and the rationale for the methods. This was something which my Mum didn't explain very much as she often cooked by experience and according to tradition. In explaining techniques, I hope that you can understand better why you are cooking in a particular way and know how to make the necessary adaptations when you make mistakes or when certain ingredients are not available. For example, what should you do if your Char Siew is too salty? Since salt is highly water-soluble you can soak the meat in water for a few minutes to rescue your dish.

If you are missing certain ingredients, can they be dropped? It depends. Some shape the heart of the dish. Others are less essential and substitutes can be used or they can be left out completely. It is not worth the stress and trouble to make a trip out just to get a non-essential ingredient. Read the introduction to each recipe to get a sense of what the key ingredients are for each dish.

The number of diners you cook for and hence the difference in quantity given in a recipe will affect the outcome. You may imagine that if the required serving is quadruple the recipe, you should, for example, use four times the amount of salt. This scaling up is not as simple as it may seem. This is why you need to taste along the way and make adjustments carefully.

I need to add a word about the pictures in this book. They play less a role to attract you to the recipes but more to give you a visual reference of what the results should look like. As an avid user of cookbooks I am always more interested in what is in the dish than what is put around it as decoration. You can tell a lot just by looking at the food. The more experienced you are, the more information you can glean about its flavours, texture and how it was prepared.

As you try the recipes, you will find that some are like old friends whom you return to again and again. Others, to begin with, may be foreign to your taste and style such that you are never quite sure where you are going with the recipe. Thus, if I can inspire you to cook some of the dishes – familiar or new – regularly, I would have done my part.

Good cookbooks should be tattered from regular use. They should have your scribbled cooking notes and highlights marked on them. Years later, your grown-up children, in learning to cook, will find your well-used books useful. I hope this cookbook will be a trusted companion and, over time, become a useful resource for you and your family.

COOKING WITHOUT RECIPES

A GOOD COOK learns new recipes so that he can learn to cook without one. This may sound like a oxymoron but the holy grail of culinary skill is versatility – to be able to cook with anything you are presented with. This was how my Mum used to cook dinners daily. She often surprised us with unfamiliar dishes concocted from whatever ingredients she could gather from the fridge or pantry.

Learning this skill – and gathering the confidence to acquire it – is necessary for the urban home cook, who is often faced with limited time, along with limited ingredients in the fridge.

Recipes have a way of confining your perspective and restricting your choices when it comes to preparing meals. Reading a recipe, you may think that you cannot produce the dish unless you have the fixed set of stated ingredients. Or you end up cooking the same dish over and over again, ignoring the myriad of combinations possible within the diversity of our rich and flavourful Asian produce.

It is also about using whatever you have. The cabbage rots away in your fridge because you cannot think of a "recipe" to cook it with. Waste not, want not. Whether in a restaurant or home kitchen, produce should never be discarded or left to rot.

One way of learning to cook without recipes is to improvise on the recipes you are familiar with. Drop or add an ingredient or two. Experiment. I also learn a lot by observing what I am eating in someone else's home or in a restaurant. Each cook has his or her own signature accent. Encountering an unusual combination often makes me think: "Well, why not?"

One can also learn a lot from other cuisines, which accentuate different ingredients and combinations. From Japanese cuisine, I have learnt that no ingredient should be seen as inferior. When everything is well prepared, even a simple or cheap ingredient like carrot can be spectacular. From Thai cuisine, I have observed that a few flavourful ingredients, forming a paste, can be used as a base for many flavourful dishes. Little is wasted in Thai cooking, including coriander roots.

MY MUM'S COOKING COMPANION FOK CHAW HENG, WHOM WE CALL HAR JIE, COOKS INSTINCTIVELY.

Cantonese cooking commonly employs stock making, drawing out the flavours from discards like bones and poorer cuts of meat. Malays have a way with *rempah*, the base for countless dishes. Leftover herbs can be used in Nasi Ulam and less-than-fresh cucumber can be pickled. Salads – whether Western, Thai or Malay/Nonya (i.e *kerabu*) – have countless combinations as long as you understand flavours and textures of the ingredients within each cuisine.

Can *bok choy* (Chinese cabbage) pair with green beans? Well, dice them up and you have a medley of diced veg to cook with. You have some cheap grass-fed steak in your fridge? Don't go Western and come up with an inferior steak dish. Instead, go oriental with some sweet tomato-based sauce and serve it with rice. It turns into a superior beef-based meal. Eggs are always around and even the simple fried egg can be appetising. If you have leftover rice, cook Fried Rice. The recipe? It is written all over your fridge and pantry. You have ginger? It is a very versatile and exotic spice which can be used for any fish or meat dish. And I mean, any. Can you think of any type of fish, or even meat, which doesn't go well with ginger?

Try using whatever you have in your fridge and pantry and surprise your family with unusual combinations. The list of dishes you can conjure up is endless. You be your own judge. If it is good, you have gained some positive experience. If not, figure out why and learn from that experience.

One reason why I explain so much in my recipes is to invite you to think deeper about what you are doing every step of the way. As you gain experience, you will find greater confidence to adapt or create your own recipes on the fly.

If you want dinner regularly on your table in today's urban, stressful and busy context, you will do well to learn to cook without recipes. I don't deny that there are days when you just don't feel like cooking after a stressful day of work, but with experience, you can still come up with something simple and delicious.

It beats takeaways any time.

THE JOY OF COMMUNITY COOKING

YOU KNOW THE KITCHEN is waking up when you hear the steady thump of the *lesong* and clash of the chopper against a wooden chopping board. If pork ribs are being chopped, loud, irregular thuds are produced. If shallots are being diced, you will hear, instead, a quieter, hypnotic drumming. And there is always a cadence that rings from the sharpening of knives

Yes, sounds of the kitchen are music to my ears. I grew up with them.

For all the glories of music, you cannot smell it. Here is where the kitchen experience is a multi-sensory one. The melody of lemongrass, shallots, mint and turmeric being pounded turns the kitchen into a symphony of scents. When the *rempah* is simmering, you can smell it from your bedroom. When the prawn noodle broth is being brewed, the smell wafts down the street and awakens the taste buds of your neighbours.

And then, there are the sounds of people. I have very fond memories of my Mum and aunties in the kitchen. Laughter. Gossip. Chatter.

As the youngest in the kitchen, I had to stay alert to instructions at all times. "Ah Choong this and Ah Choong that." The bowl needs to be washed. Leaves need to be separated from stems. Prawns need to be shelled. The tables need to be wiped. The food in the wok needs to be tossed. The herbs in the *lesong* need to be pounded. All the tasks were simple, requiring little skill – but this was how I was first taught to cook. The food on the table starts with the *lesong* on the kitchen floor. Indeed, kitchen enculturation is the best way to pick up food preparation and cooking skills.

I have a chance to relive community cooking in the churches I have served in as a pastor. I enjoyed cooking with the Food Ministry folks at St James' Church where I served for 14 years. Lucy Kwok, a colleague and close family friend, is a joy to cook with. I have learnt from her, along with other housewives, some finer points of cooking that I was previously unaware of. Humility is the key to learning and cooking tips can be gained when you are cooking with other cooks.

We enjoyed the experience of cooking for large groups, for special occasions and events such

I HAD MANY YEARS OF COMMUNITY COOKING WITH THE FOOD MINISTRY TEAM AT ST JAMES' CHURCH. HERE, I AM WITH LUCY KWOK PREPARING TO SERVE NASI LEMAK AT AN ALPHA COURSE DINNER.

as The Alpha Course. In busy Singapore, catering ("outsourcing") is often necessary but it is great to rally together those who are passionate about home cooking to do something for the community. Passion is contagious – through the process, we have learnt a lot and had a lot of fun. Cooking for a large group is hard work but it is always satisfying to see others enjoying your food. A cook, like any artist, needs an audience. It was our privilege to have appreciative ones.

When I was posted to St Andrew's Cathedral, my experience of community cooking continued in earnest. I was amazed at the skill and passion of many members from a variety of ethnic backgrounds when it came to kitchen craft. Apart from Singapore cuisine, we have also enjoyed cooking and eating delicious Sri Lankan, Korean and Indian meals together. My Korean friends are amazed by Nasi Ulam. In turn, we are amazed by pickled Kimchi. My Sri Lankan members whip up some amazing vegetable dishes, cooking it patiently in small batches, resulting in a perfect texture which is hard to achieve in commercial cooking. Undoubtedly, anonymous home cooks are the true celebrities of any cuisine.

I have discovered that home cooks love to share their cooking with others. Some are reticent about introducing their "humble" dishes to the wider community, and need encouragement to do so. But once confidence is gained and joy experienced, there is no turning back.

I would love to see many churches and other communities in Singapore rediscovering the joy of community, gathered around a simple home-cooked spread. Here is an important part of our culture and heritage to retain, amidst trends of commercialisation, globalisation and "Michelinisation" of our food heritage.

ABOVE: HAR JIE TEACHING (FROM LEFT) , NITA, BELLE, FE, LUCY KWOK AND WENDY LAM HOW TO MAKE CURRY PUFFS.

LEFT: MAMA, MY FATHER'S FIRST WIFE, GOT ALONG VERY WELL WITH MY MOTHER, AND SHE OFTEN HELPED MUM WHEN SHE COOKED. HERE, SHE IS HELPING TO PREPARE HAKKA YONG TAU FOO FOR A CHURCH EVENT

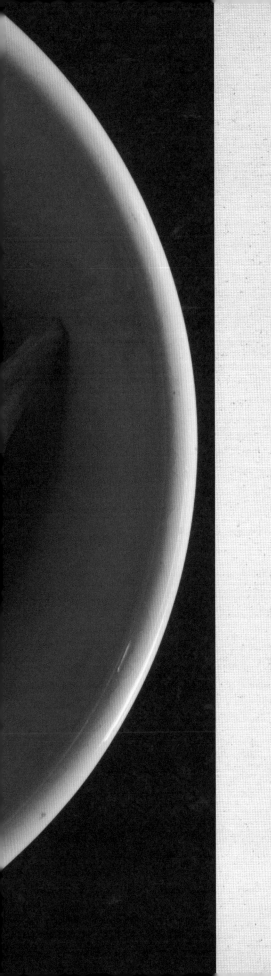

POULTRY

SI YAU KAI
Soy Sauce Chicken

Si Yau Kai is a well-loved traditional Chinese dish which has stood the test of time.

The chicken is gently braised whole in a soy-based sauce. Then, it is skillfully sliced, keeping the flavourful skin on, and eaten with rice along with sides like hard-boiled eggs and *tau korn* (firm bean curd) which have been cooked and marinated in the same sauce. For Si Yau Kai, the soy-flavoured skin is the main highlight of this dish.

Food stalls which sell this will use the sauce over and over again to cook their daily batches of chicken. They call it the Thousand Year Sauce. You can imagine how the flavours will develop over time.

You can do the same at home, and the same sauce can also be used to braise duck.

The most common approach is to use a deep pot or wok to braise the chicken. Alternatively, you can use an electric rice cooker or a *sous vide* enabler to control the temperature.

What type of chicken should you use? The kampong, bare-necked or free-range chicken are best as their skin is thicker and harder to break during cooking. If you use a white broiler, choose a larger one which has more flavour. For the home dinner, you can also use a whole thigh or parts of a chicken. This way you, need less sauce for braising.

Your sauce is, of course, all important. Start with a good brand of soy sauce. As for aromatics, there are many options. Think white peppercorn, cinnamon bark, and star anise for a start. If you can get your hands on them, dried orange peel and licorice sticks (*kum cho*) will add a fruity and unique fragrance.

This dish makes a complete meal when you serve it with firm beancurd (*tau korn*) and hard-boiled eggs with cucumber and fresh coriander leaves. It makes for an attractive and appetizing spread.

The great thing about this dish is after you have made the sauce, it can be reused. Boil the sauce before you keep it in the fridge. The second time round will be easier as the sauce is well flavoured and good to go. You can also use the sauce to braise pork belly, pork trotters or peanuts.

Si Yau Kai

SERVES 4-6

1 large chicken
 (1.5 kg or 3.3 lb upwards)

2 tbsps oil
2 stalks spring onions, cut into
 5-cm (2-in) lengths
1 sprig coriander leaves
3 star anise
1 cinnamon stick
1 black cardamon
3 dried orange peels (optional)
10 white peppercorns, crushed
2 licorice sticks (*kum cho*)
 (optional)
20 cloves garlic, lightly bruised
7½ cm (3 in) ginger, lightly
 crushed
400 ml (1.7 cups) light soy sauce
100 ml (0.4 cup) thick dark soy
 sauce
100 g (3.5 oz) rock sugar
1 litre (4 cups) water
3 pieces firm beancurd
 (*tau korn*)
6 eggs, hard boiled
2 cucumbers, sliced
Fried shallots

Garnish
Coriander leaves
Fried shallots

Heat up a pot or wok. Add the oil, spring onions, coriander root, spices, garlic, ginger and fry for about 2 minutes.

Pour in the sauces and, when they are heated up, put in the rock sugar. Stir to dissolve before putting in the whole chicken. Add enough water to ensure that the chicken is covered. Let it simmer over low fire for 40 minutes. If you are using a wok, you may not be able to cover the chicken with the braising liquid. In which case, you will need to turn the chicken over from time to time.

Take the chicken out and let it rest till it comes down to room temperature. At this stage, it is still gently cooking inside. To test whether the chicken is cooked, stick something sharp into the thigh meat. If the juice runs clear, it is done. What you do not want to do is to overcook the chicken. A tell-tale sign is the skin tearing at the wings or other parts of the chicken (due to heat, not poor handling).

Transfer some of the sauce into another pot. Heat it up and add the firm beancurd and hard boiled eggs. Braise for 15 minutes and switch off the fire. Let them steep in the sauce till you are ready to serve the dish.

Return the cooked chicken to the remainder of the braising sauce to let it soak in the flavours.

You will need to strain the finished gravy to remove the residual bits. When using the sauce as gravy, you can adjust the taste further by adding some sugar, as a sweeter sauce goes well with the chicken.

Chop the chicken for serving. After all the careful cooking to keep the skin perfect, you don't want to mess it up. Use a sharp cleaver. Cut off the thighs and wings first before cutting the body into large pieces. Flatten the pieces first with the flat side of your cleaver – give it a smack.

FACING: SOME OF THE HERBS AND SPICES USED TO FLAVOUR THE SAUCE. USE WHAT YOU HAVE AS THERE IS NO FIXED LIST OF FLAVOURINGS FOR THE RECIPE.

AYAM GORENG REMPAH
Fried Spiced Chicken

Fried chicken is universally loved. We have all been introduced to the American Southern Fried Chicken varieties through fast-food restaurants.

That said, since young, I have always been attracted to the Ayam Goreng made by the *makcik* (Malay for 'aunt') in Nasi Padang stalls. While it does not use a thick batter, it is crispy, with the pronounced taste of turmeric and other spices. It is delicious eaten with rice and sambal. It also fits very well in a Nasi Lemak spread (page 201).

The first step in making Ayam Goreng is marinating the chicken. Use ground spices – the fresher they are, the better.

As for the chicken, use the free-range kampong chicken or the bare-necked French variety. The white or breast meat is tastier and has a nice, flaky texture. If these are not available, use larger broilers as they are older and thus, tastier. If I am using just drumsticks or thighs, I will normally go for parts from a white broiler as its dark meat is not so tough.

If you are using a whole chicken, cut it into 10 or 12 pieces. The drumsticks and wings should be kept whole. Larger cuts help to keep the meat moist inside with a crisp exterior as you deep fry.

As I am not making a thick crust, unlike for Southern Fried Chicken, I do not use a thick batter. Just coat the chicken with cornflour lightly before frying.

From my experience, Ayam Goreng is the first to go in a dinner spread. So, there is no harm cooking more as leftovers keep well.

Ayam Goreng Rempah

1.5-2 kg (3.3-4.4 lb) chicken,
 cut into 14 -16 large pieces
Oil for deep frying

Marinade
2 tsps coriander powder
1 tsp cumin powder
1 tsp fennel powder
2 tsps turmeric powder
2 tsps white pepper powder
2 tsps chilli powder
200 ml (0.8 cup) coconut milk
2 tsps salt
3 tbsps cornflour

Preparation
Warm up the coconut milk in a pot and add the ground spices and the rest of the marinade ingredients. When the marinade has cooled, marinate the chicken pieces overnight or for at least 4 hours.

Cooking
Heat up enough oil for deep frying in a wok or an electric fryer. Use vegetable oil for its higher smoking point. 325°F (160°C) is the ideal temperature. In traditional Malay cooking, no one uses a thermometer. From experience, you can see when the oil starts to churn. Or you can drop in a bit of dough and see if it sizzles. My method is to put my palm above the oil and once it's unbearably hot, I know it is ready. However, the oil should not be smoking hot. That said, if it is not hot enough, the chicken will not fry properly and be soggy.

Coat the chicken lightly in cornflour and deep fry them in small batches of about 4-5 pieces till they turn golden brown. Breast meat will take 7-8 minutes, depending on the size. Thigh meat will generally need about 2 minutes more. For this reason, I sometimes separate the thigh and breast meat and fry them separately.

Remove the chicken pieces and place them on a colander or rack to drain the oil.

Dredge the oil in between batches to keep the oil clean and to avoid having the crumbs competing for the heat as you fry the chicken.

If you are serving the fried chicken some time after cooking, keep them warm in the oven. You can also give them another quick fry to crisp them up again before you serve.

FRIED CHICKEN WINGS

Fried chicken wings are delicious and everyone's favourite snack. They are great for parties as finger food or as an appetizer – and both adults and kids love them. They are also suitable as one of the dishes for your rice-based daily dinners. And did I mention that they are also easy on the pocket? These may be the reasons why my Mum made them so regularly.

This recipe is one of Mum's favourite ways of doing chicken wings. But there are many other ways which you can marinate them. For example, try using dark soy sauce, light soy sauce, cooking wine and some cornflour as a marinade. You will be surprised how delicious this can be as well.

1 kg (2.2 lbs) chicken wings	Marinate the chicken wings with the marinade and keep in the fridge till it is ready to be fried.
Marinade	
2 tsps salt	Mix the batter ingredients to make a smooth batter.
1 tsp sugar	
2 tsps Chinese wine	Heat up oil in a wok for deep frying. Dip the chicken wings
2 tsps mustard powder	in the batter and deep fry in batches for about 3 minutes
2 tsps pepper	till golden. Remember to drain the oil from the cooked wings on paper kitchen towels.
Batter	
4 tbsps plain flour	Note:
2 tbsps rice flour	I will sometimes add a teaspoon of Eno fruit salt into the
2 tbsps cornflour	batter. Composed basically of baking soda and citric acid,
480 ml (2 cups) water	Eno helps the batter stay crispy for a longer time.
½ tsp salt	
½ tsp five-spice powder	
½ tsp pepper	
Oil for deep frying	

AYAM GORENG HALIA
Fried Ginger Chicken

This is another Malay fried chicken recipe. It is similar to the Indonesian Ayam Garuda.

It uses three types of ginger – old ginger, blue ginger and turmeric. The blended ginger will crisp up when fried, adding flavour and texture.

Just remember that ginger is acidic, and if you marinate the chicken with it for too long, the meat will become mushy. Don't marinate it for more than 30 minutes.

I often pair this dish with Nasi Ulam (page 197). It also goes well with plain rice and Sambal Belacan. If you add deep-fried firm beancurd (*tau korn*), fresh lettuce and give the fried chicken a whack before you serve it, you have something akin to Ayam Penyet!

1.5 - 2 kg (3.3 - 4.4 lb) chicken, cut into 12 pieces 2 tsps salt 1 tsp sugar 3 tbsps cornflour Oil for deep frying	Grind or pound the gingers and lemongrass. Add salt, sugar and cornflour to the ground ginger and mix. Marinate the chicken in this mixture for 30 minutes.
Marinade 15 cm (6 in) old ginger 1 thumb-size turmeric 3 lemongrass bulbs 5 cm (2 in) blue ginger (galangal, *lengkuas*)	Heat up the oil in a wok or deep pan. Deep fry the chicken pieces for 7-8 minutes, turning or moving them around occasionally to prevent spot burning. Use a strainer to scoop up the fried ginger floss. These are delicious. Deep fry the remaining ginger paste in the marinade to make more ginger floss. Use the floss to garnish the dish.

DEEP FRYING, PAN FRYING & SHALLOW FRYING

THE DEEP FRYING technique is shunned by some due to the perception that deep-fried food is unhealthy, and that the cooking process can release oily fumes which make the kitchen dirty. However, with care, it is possible to minimize these disadvantages.

The purpose of deep frying is to make the food crispy, especially the exterior, and yet ensure it is not burnt. You also want the meat to be tender and moist.

For deep frying in Asian cooking, we don't bother about measuring the temperature of the oil. We just watch for signs like 'shimmering in the oil' or, often, we just put in a bit of food or poke a chopstick in and look out for bubbles. If the oil is smoky, it is over heated. With time, the cook will get a good sense from looking at the oil and hearing the sound to know if the oil is properly heated. I put my hand a few inches above the oil (I don't recommend dipping it in!) to sense the heat. When it is uncomfortably hot, I know the oil is ready.

When the oil is hot enough, you hear a sizzling sound and see bubbles. That is air and water interacting with the hot oil. The bubbles form a cushion around the food, resulting in minimal absorption of oil and creating a crisped crust from the air pressure. Thus, if the oil is not hot enough, you have a 'soaking in oil' effect. Likewise, if you leave the food in there for too long, after the moisture has escaped from the food, the vacuum created will suck in the oil. The same thing happens if you do not drain fried food properly.

How long should you leave the food to cook in the oil? Once the sizzling slows down, it is a sign that the moisture has escaped from the food. And if you have done it right, it should be perfectly crispy by then.

As the food is being deep fried, bits of it will remain in the oil and compete for the heat as you fry a new batch. These bits will also be burnt in the oil, making your food taste bitter. So, after every batch of frying, the oil should be dredged. I should add that the electric fryer, which is common in commercial use, is better than using a wok over a stove fire. It is more consistent and efficient and I recommend using it if you deep fry your food regularly.

There is the need to drain the oil off deep fried food. In fact, this may be the most important thing to do. It comes after frying and often, a careless cook will do it as an afterthought or neglect the step altogether. The best way to drain oil is to use a colander or strainer with large gaps and leave the fried food there with a bowl underneath it to collect the dripping oil.

Pan frying uses direct contact of the food with the hot metal of the wok or pan to ensure that high heat is quickly transferred to the surface of the food to cook it. This is the technique for cooking steaks. The marinade or sauce will stay on the food, forming a flavourful crust, in contrast to dissipation into the oil through deep frying. The recipes for Fried Assam Prawn (page 97) and Pan-fried Turmeric Mackerel (page 117) use this technique.

This is a good alternative to deep frying when you want to control the amount of oil used, or when you are cooking a small amount of food and do not want to bother with setting up for deep-frying.

Shallow frying in a wok is another good way of frying fish and this is the technique used for Chilli Fish (page 113). This uses more oil than pan frying but less than deep frying. The fish sits on the wok and is partially submerged in the oil. Turn the fish at the half-way mark to ensure evenness in the cooking.

NONYA CHICKEN CURRY

I know I am biased. Every boy grows up loving the curry his Mum made and I am no exception. Mum's version is the best. I have memories of eating it with white bread, sucking clean every bone and wiping up every bit of the curry. Hers is a Nonya version and it is sometimes called Curry Kapitan.

These are the reason why I like it:

The meat is cooked just right; firm and yet tender to the bite. If you see the meat falling off the bone, it is a clear sign that the curry is overcooked and that won't be my mum's.

There is sufficient oil in the curry which adds to its smooth mouth-feel. It is supposed to be a curry, not soup. Her curry is drier and not swimming in coconut milk.

The wonderful fragrance of spices and herbs is a clear sign that the curry was made from fresh spices and herbs.

Let's start with some basics about what makes for a good curry.

You need a good-tasting chicken. I normally get the fresh ones from the wet market and avoid the frozen variety from the supermarts. Free-range chicken will, of course, taste better.

Spices need to be fresh. Use fresh spice powder mix or toast and grind seeds. As for chilli paste, I will normally make paste from dried chilies or buy ready-made fresh paste from the market.

Shallots are essential to give body to this curry. The smaller, pointed variety of shallots are the sweetest. The use of candlenut (*buah keras*) is to add a nutty taste and texture. Other kinds of nuts can be used too.

As for potatoes, get the yellow fleshed ones, please. They are tastier and have a nice, crumbly texture.

A wok or a wide-mouthed, traditional curry claypot will work well for cooking this dish, ensuring even cooking throughout and a curry that's thickened through condensation.

As you can imagine, if accompanied by a veg like cucumber and bread or rice at the dining table, this chicken curry is a complete meal.

Nonya Chicken Curry

1½ kg (3.3 lb) chicken
3 lemongrass bulbs
20 shallots
10 cloves garlic
1 tbsp chopped turmeric
30 dried chillies
1 kg (2.2 lbs) potato
10 candlenuts (*buah keras*)

240 ml (1 cup) cooking oil
2 tbsps salt
1 tbsp sugar
240 ml (1 cup) water
1 sprig curry leaves
200 ml (0.8 cup) coconut milk

Dry spices
2 star anise
2 cinnamon sticks
2 tsps coriander powder or seeds
1 tsp cumin powder or seeds

Preparation

Clean out the inside of the chicken thoroughly. Cut the chicken into medium to small pieces. Keep the fat.

If using seed spices, toast the coriander and cumin seeds on a dry pan and grind to a powder. If you have some fresh cumin and coriander powder, use them.

Blend the bulbs of the lemongrass, shallot, candlenuts, garlic, and turmeric finely.

Soak the dried chillies in warm water for 15 minutes and blend finely.

Peel the potatoes and cut into about 2½-cm chunks.

Cooking the curry

Heat up the oil in a wok or wide, deep pot, then add the blended spice paste, dry spices and chilli paste.

Simmer on low flame for 20 minutes. Stir to ensure there is no bottom burning. If needed, add some water to bring down the heat and add moisture to the simmering paste. Add half the salt and sugar.

Put in the chicken and stir. Add the 240 ml of water and simmer. After 10 minutes, add the potatoes and curry leaves. Stir occasionally to ensure there is no bottom burning.

Then, add the coconut milk. Taste and adjust with salt and sugar according to what you like.

After about 40 minutes of cooking, the chicken meat should be done.

If the chicken has lots of fat, there may be too much oil for your liking. Just remove some and keep it for use on another occasion.

STEAMED CHICKEN IN GINGER SAUCE

Free-range or kampong chicken is great for steaming. The breed I like to use is the bare-necked chicken which originates from France where it is known as Poulet Rouge. Compared to the white broiler, its skin is thicker, the meat firmer and has more flavour.

Ask the chicken seller to chop it into bite-sized pieces for you. As a guide, the chicken wing should be cut into five parts: Drumstick into two, mid-wings into two, and the wing tip.

The ginger sauce is prepared beforehand and can be kept refridgerated till required. I use a combination of old and young ginger. If you can get the strong and fragrant Bentong ginger from Malaysia, use it. Dicing instead of blending or pounding the ginger will result in a cleaner and less fiberous texture..

Cornflour will help to give the meat a smooth, silken texture when cooked. As always, steam your meat in a single layer.

This dish is best served with other dishes which are milder in taste or *ching*, as we will say in Cantonese and Mandarin. It won't go well with another strong dish like curry.

1 kampong or free-range chicken (about 1.5 kg, 3.3 lb), chopped into bite-sized pieces
2 tbsps cornflour
1 tsp salt
2 tbsps Shaoxing rice wine or Chinese rose wine
Coriander leaves or spring onions, chopped

Ginger sauce
5 tbsps diced old ginger
3 tbsps diced young ginger
3 tbsps diced garlic
3 tbsps sesame oil
3 tbsps cooking oil
2 tbsps oyster sauce
2 tbsps soy sauce
1 tbsp sugar

Note: The ginger sauce also goes well with steamed pork ribs or fish.

Preparing the ginger sauce
Chop the young ginger with a sharp cleaver, knife or electric chopper. Squeeze out the juice from the ginger. Dice the garlic.

Combine the sesame oil and cooking oil and heat in a wok over a small flame. Add the garlic and, when it has browned, add the ginger pastes. Simmer for 10 minutes, stirring periodically to ensure that the paste is not burned.

Add the oyster sauce, soy sauce, and sugar and simmer for another 10 minutes. Adjust the taste to your liking by adding soy sauce or sugar.

Steaming the chicken
Marinate the chicken pieces with cornflour, salt and wine for about 30 minutes in a steaming tray.

Just before steaming, mix in the ginger sauce. As ginger is acidic, marinating the chicken in it for too long will turn the meat mushy.

Steam for 12 minutes on high heat. Transfer onto a serving plate, garnish with coriander leaves or spring onions. Serve immediately.

STEAMED EGG

Steamed egg brings back many childhood memories. It is comfort food at its best.

As it is quick and easy to make, mothers will feed their children with it. When the rice cooker button pops up from 'cook' to 'warm', my Mum put a plate on the rice. She poured an egg-water mixture into the plate, closed the lid, and let it steam for a few minutes. It is an efficient way of cooking, making use of the steam and heat from the cooked rice. Sprinkle on some diced spring onions to introduce some veg to the child's diet.

For every egg you use, you add an equal amount of water – 1:1 ratio. Use the egg shell to measure the water. Make a hole at the sharper end of the egg by giving it a light tap with a spoon and peel the top off.

If the mixture is shallow in the plate, no more than a centimeter, it should be perfectly cooked in 7 minutes. This is the key to avoid an overcooked steamed egg with pock marks: keep the egg mixture shallow. When steaming, use medium fire.

To test if it is done after 7 minutes, rest the tip of a chopstick in the middle of the custard. If it feels firm, it is done. Just experiment and you will get the hang of it. The worse thing that can happen is overcooking it, resulting in some pock marks on the surface. But that's no disaster as you can still eat it.

Serve the custard with a sauce on top – light soy sauce, sesame oil and even some fish sauce. Or use leftover chicken stock, if you have any. Alternatively, pour in a bottle of chicken essence with some soy sauce added. Include diced spring onions and fried shallots. Sprinkle on some white pepper.

If you want a lighter texture, use more water. Replacing water with soy bean milk will give a heavier texture akin to tofu.

This dish is best eaten immediately after you take it out of the steamer.

5 eggs **Equivalent volume of water**	Mix the egg and water. Break the yolks and stir briefly. Strain to remove the white clumps of membrane.
Sauce 2 tbsps light soy sauce ½ tbsp sesame oil or onion oil 2 tbsps chicken stock or chicken essence (optional)	Pour into a shallow dish. Ensure that the mixture is no more than 1 cm (0.4 in) deep. Heat up the steamer over medium fire and steam the eggy mixture. It will be done after 7 minutes.
Garnish Dashes of white pepper Diced spring onions Fried shallots	Meanwhile, mix the sauces together. Remove the custard from steamer, add the sauce, the diced spring onions, fried shallots and dashes of white pepper. Serve immediately.

KUNG PO CHICKEN
Chicken Stir Fried with Cashews and Chillies

If you pick up a typical Chinese cookbook, you will find that the ingredients in many stir fry recipes are very similar. You will find the usual suspects: soy sauce, sesame oil, Shaoxing or Chinese rice wine, oyster sauce and so on. One teaspoon of this and two teaspoons of that.

This is not a criticism of stir fry recipes. It is good to know that the same few sauces can be used over and over again, with slight variations, to create so many different dishes. For this reason, I believe that a good Chinese home kitchen should have bottles of good quality sauces.

An underrated sauce in some kitchens is black vinegar. This should surprise us given how often balsamic vinegar is used in Italian and Western dishes. Dashes of some good quality black vinegar can make a significant difference to many stir-fry dishes.

This is a simple dish which can be easily cooked for your everyday dinners.

500 g (1.1 lb) deboned chicken
   thigh, cut into strips
20 dried chillies
1 tsp cornflour
3 tbsps water
3 tbsps oil
200 g (7 oz) cashew nuts
1 tsp chopped garlic
10 slices ginger
3 stalks spring onion, cut into
   2½-cm (1-in) lengths
Chinese rice wine to taste

Sauce
1 tsp black soy sauce
2 tbsps soy sauce
2 tsps sweet soy sauce,
   kecap manis or sugar
2 tsps black vinegar
1 tsp sesame oil
1 tbsp cornflour

Mix the ingredients for the sauce in a bowl. This way, you can taste it and adjust it to your liking.

Marinate the chicken in the sauce for at least half an hour.

Rehydrate the dried chillies in warm water for about 15 minutes. Remove the seeds to reduce spiciness if you wish. Drain.

Mix the cornflour with 3 tablespoons of water and set aside.

Heat up the oil in the wok. Gently stir and cook the cashew nuts over low heat till they are light brown, about 5 minutes. Set aside the nuts.

Using the same oil, add the drained dried chillies and fry for about a minute. Then put in the garlic and ginger and stir fry for another minute.

Increase the fire to medium and add the chicken along with the remaining sauce. Stir every 3 minutes to ensure that the chicken is not burnt. The chicken should be cooked after about 15 minutes.

Add the roasted cashew nuts and the water-cornflour mixture to thicken the sauce. Finish off with dashes of rice wine. Top with the spring onions, stir it briefly and serve immediately.

STIR FRIED GINGER CHICKEN

This is a dish I learned from my Mum and one which I cooked regularly when I first began to do some home-cooking soon after I graduated from varsity. The years went by, and as I learned more recipes and got more confident in cooking, I hardly served this dish.

But like a long-forgotten friend, it is good to cook it once in a while, especially since my family loves it. My wife always likes some sauce with her rice and my girls like plain chicken dishes. So, this is a very agreeable dish for my home – one which I go to when I run out of ideas!

If you marinate the meat beforehand with some cornflour, it will help to make it smoother and more succulent.

1 chicken, cut into serving pieces
20 slices young ginger
3 cloves garlic, chopped
1 tbsp oyster sauce
1 tsp dark soy sauce
2 tsps premium light soy sauce
2 cups water
1 tbsp Chinese rice wine
6 stalks spring onions, cut into
   5-cm (2 in) strips
3 tbsps cooking oil

Marinade
1 tbsp cornflour
2 tsps light soy sauce

Marinate the chicken in the cornflour and light soy sauce for 30 minutes.

Heat up the oil in a wok.

Add the ginger slices and stir fry for 2 minutes.

Then add the garlic. When the garlic turns lightly brown, add the chicken and stir fry for 1 minute. Add the sauces and continue to stir fry for another minute. Then add the water and let the dish simmer with the wok covered for 20 minutes. Stir occasionally to prevent bottom burning.

Add the rice wine and spring onions. Stir fry for one minute more.

Serve it warm. This dish can also be cooked and served in a claypot.

MEAT

COFFEE PORK RIBS

Who would have thought that pork and coffee could go together? Yet, Coffee Pork Ribs is a common menu item in *cze char* (literally "cooking and frying" in Hokkien) stalls in Singapore and Malaysia.

The meat needs to be tenderized in a marinade beforehand. Then it is deep fried and set aside. Next, the sauce is prepared and the pork thrown back in for coating before serving.

Marinade, deep fry and then sauce it. It is a simple three-stage cooking and this is why the method is popular with *cze char* cooks.

Sodium bicarbonate or baking soda, widely used to bake cakes, is added to the marinade to tenderize the meat. Don't be hung up about using it. A teaspoon will do for a kilogram of ribs.

Deep frying the pork is the step where the ribs are cooked, of course. It also caramelises the pork and gives a beautiful colour.

The coffee for the sauce can come from instant granules or espresso from your coffee machine pods. The intensity of the sauce depends on your preference.

You can substitute other kinds of sauces such as Jing Du, plum sauce or sweet and sour sauce in this recipe.

Marinade
1 kg (2.2 lb) pork ribs
3 tbsps light soy sauce
1 tsp sugar
1 tsp sesame oil
1 tbsp Chinese wine or brandy
1 tsp sodium bicarbonate
Cornflour

Sauce
2 tbsps instant coffee granules
2 tbsp Worcestershire Sauce
2 tbsps oil
1 tsp dark soy sauce
1 tbsp sugar
1 tbsp Chinese wine
1 tsp cornflour mixed in
  ½ cup of water

Garnish
Coriander leaves
Chilli strips

Cut the ribs into small pieces of about 2½ cm (1 in). The butcher can do this for you.

Marinate the ribs for an hour. Strain the ribs to remove excess liquid then coat it lightly with some cornflour.

Deep fry the ribs till they are golden brown and set aside. If you are using coffee granules for the sauce, dissolve them in some hot water.

Mix the ingredients for the sauce. Heat up the oil in a wok over a small flame and add the mixture. When the sauce has thickened, add the ribs and toss.

Serve them hot, garnished with coriander leaves and the chilli strips.

NONYA PORK RIB CURRY

Pork curries are of course non-existent in Malay cuisine but it is popular in that of Nonya and Thai. Some Thai curries use tender cuts and the cooking is quick. Tougher pork cuts are also delicious when braised for a longer time so that the flavours of the spices and meat meld together.

Pork ribs are great for this method and the eating experience is enhanced as you bite into the curried meat around the bone; both giving the sweet flavour of the sauce.

In a perfect Pork Rib Curry, the meat should not fall off the bone but is yet tender to the bite. As pork rib cuts can vary in muscle and fat content, you need to ensure it is cooked till it is tender. Bone is a bad conductor of heat and this is why you need to cook pork ribs a bit longer compared to boneless cuts.

How much spice and how intense you want the curry to be is up to you. I will say that sugar is not necessary as pork ribs are naturally sweet. And yes, if your ribs have fat on them, don't trim them off. It will be like making scones without butter.

2 kg (4.4 lbs) pork ribs
500 g (1.1 lb) red onions, peeled
200 g (7 oz) garlic, peeled
3 lemongrass bulbs
240 ml (1 cup) cooking oil
3 tbsps curry powder
1 tsp turmeric powder
2 tbsps chilli powder or paste
1 tbsp salt, or to taste
1 sprig curry leaves
240 ml (1 cup) coconut milk
200 ml (0.8 cup) water
1 kg (2.2 lb) yellow potatoes, peeled

Cut the pork ribs into equal bite-size pieces. You could ask the butcher to do this for you.

Blend the peeled onions, garlic and lemongrass bulbs together into a paste.

Heat up the oil in the wok or pot over a low fire. Add the inion, garlic and lemongrass paste. Stir, then add the curry, turmeric and chilli powders and salt. Put in the curry leaves and simmer for about 15 minutes.

Add the pork ribs and stir. After 5 minutes, add the coconut milk and water. Simmer. It will take about an hour to cook the ribs but adjust the cooking time so that the meat is not tough yet does not fall off the bone either, a sign that it is overcooked.

At the mid-point of cooking, after about 30 minutes, add the peeled potatoes.

Skim off the oil before serving. The oil is flavourful and can be kept for another batch of curry or sambal.

STEAMED PORK RIBS WITH PLUM SAUCE

My Mum cooked this very often. It is quick and easy to do. In smaller portions, it can be placed on a steel plate and steamed in a rice cooker by putting it on top of the rice.

The cuts with soft bones are best for this dish as the meat is tender and suited for steaming. Some cuts are tougher, which means you need to marinade it with some bicarbonate of soda. The cornflour will thicken the sauce and add a silky texture to the meat.

Remember to get the butcher to cut the pork ribs into small pieces of about 2½ cm (1 in). When you steam, ensure that the pieces are all in a single layer.

Adding fermented black soy beans (*tau see*) makes a variation of this dish – Steamed Pork with Black Soy Beans – popular in *dim sum* restaurants.

1 kg (2.2 lb) soft-boned pork ribs	Marinate the pork ribs for 30 minutes.
Marinade	Steam the ribs in one layer on a shallow plate for 15 minutes on high heat.
3 tsps plum sauce	
3 tsps minced garlic	
1 tsp salt	Garnish with cut chilies and coriander leaves and serve immediately.
1 tsp sugar	
A dash of white pepper	
3 tsps cornflour	
2 tsps cooking oil	
1 tsp Shaoxing rice wine or Chinese rose wine	

Garnish
1 red chilli, sliced
Coriander leaves

BRAISED PORK RIBS IN ORANGE SAUCE

This recipe shows a simple way of cooking delicious pork ribs using a wok.

It benefits from the same convenience as the Wok-cooked Char Siew (page 75). You do not need to marinate the pork ribs beforehand. From start to finish, you cook in a wok, unlike the two-step method of deep frying and sauce-coating for Coffee Pork Ribs (page 53).

For this wok-braising method, you start by slowly braising the ribs. The ribs and sauce will caramelize towards the end.

Bones are a poor conductor of heat. So, generally, you need more time to cook ribs compared to boneless cuts like pork belly. Adding half a teaspoon of bicarbonate of soda will cut down the cooking time and help tenderise the ribs. However, if you do not like using bicarbonate of soda, just cook a bit longer. Cutting the ribs into bite-size pieces makes cooking easier and faster too.

As for flavouring, you can go in many directions: Coffee, orange, honey, *hoi sin*, and so on. For the fruity flavours, just use whatever jams you have. Orange goes well with ribs. Make a sauce, tasting and balancing it before you add it to the ribs. For the recipe below, I use honey and orange.

The timing I indicated is just a guide. While you want your pork ribs to be tender, you do not want them to be falling off the bone. As you are using a wok, it is easy to check whether the meat is done.

1 kg (2.2 lb) pork ribs, cut into
  2½-cm (1-in) pieces
2 tbsps cooking oil
240 ml (1 cup) water

Sauce
2 tbsps orange marmalade or
  240 ml (1 cup) orange juice
1 tbsp honey
1 tsp sesame oil
2 tbsps minced ginger
1 tbsp Chinese wine or liquor
1 tsp salt
1 tsp white pepper
½ tsp bicarbonate of soda
  (optional)

Garnish
Lettuce
Coriander leaves

Mix the sauce. Taste it and adjust, if necessary, to get the balance you prefer.

Heat up the oil in a wok. Add in the pork ribs and fry for about a minute.

Put in the sauce and water and let it simmer for about 40 minutes or till the ribs are tender.

Towards the end of cooking, the sauce should thicken and your ribs should start to caramelize.

Plate the ribs on a bed of lettuce and garnish with the coriander leaves.

PORK RIBS WITH BITTER GOURD & BLACK BEAN SAUCE

Most of us have a story about how we used to hate bitter gourd when we were young. As we grow up and our taste buds and receptors mature, we begin to appreciate the nuances that bitter flavours bring to our food. For some, it changes from tolerance to love for this gourd.

If you like bitter gourd, you have probably eaten it with fermented black bean (*tau see*). It is a classic combination. Interestingly, it is not sweet which balances the bitter, but the saltiness.

The one thing you need to know about bitter gourd is that it cooks fast. Texture is important and you want it to have a bit of crunch to it. Don't overcook it. I find that you hardly need more than 5 to 10 minutes to cook it just right, depending on how thinly you slice it.

Soak the sliced gourd in lightly salted water for 10 minutes to refresh it and to remove some of the bitterness.

As pork ribs go so well with fermented black beans, it makes sense to have all three together. Gently braise the pork ribs first and, towards the end, add the slices of bitter gourd.

Coming back to bitter flavours: in life, we like things sweet and good. Life as we know it, will be pretty one-dimensional if we have not encountered difficulties and suffering. In fact, the Bible talks a lot about suffering and the darker realities of life. Life, like food, sometimes need to be both sweet and bitter.

---

1 bitter gourd
1 kg (2.2 lb) pork ribs, cut into bite-size pieces
2 tbsps fermented black beans
2 tbsps cooking oil
2 tbps chopped garlic
2 tsps sugar
2 tsps dark soy sauce
2 tsps soy sauce
1 cup water

Slice the bitter gourd into rings of about ½ cm (0.2 in) in thickness.

If you are using dry fermented black beans, you may have to run them through water if they come coated with salt. Chop them up.

Heat up the oil in a wok or pot. Fry the garlic and the chopped fermented black beans. Add the ribs, sugar and the sauces. Stir-fry.

Then add a cup of water and cook the dish over very small flame and simmer with the wok covered.

If the water dries up, add some hot water. After about 30 minutes, add the slices of bitter gourd, stir and simmer it for 10 minutes. Serve immediately.

BRAISED PORK RIBS
IN GINGER & BLACK BEAN SAUCE

Ginger and fermented black soy bean paste is a wonderful combination and this, my Mum's favourite pork rib recipe, clearly shows why.

The method for this dish is similar to braising pork ribs in the wok (see page 59), except that it is wet-braised, and you are aiming for a saucy dish without the caramelization. You cook the meat till it is tender in a flavoured sauce, keeping it "slow and low" to retain the juiciness of the meat. While tender, it should still have a good bite to it.

This dish is definitely suited for daily dinners. Add another vegetable dish and rice and you will have a complete meal. And here's a bonus: the dish keeps well.

1 kg (2.2 lb) pork ribs, cut into
   2½-cm (1-in) lengths
2 tbsps oil
4 tbsps chopped ginger
1 tbsp chopped garlic
1 chilli, diced
1 tsp black soy bean sauce
   (*tau see*)
2 tsp yellow soy bean sauce
   (*tau cheong*)
200 ml (0.8 cup) water
1 tbsp sugar
1 tbsp soy sauce
1 tbsp dark soy sauce
A few stalks of spring onions,
   cut into 2½-cm (1-in) lengths
Chopped coriander stems
   and leaves.

Heat up the oil in a wok. Then put in the chopped ginger and garlic. Add half of the diced chilli, keeping the other half for garnishing.

Add the bean pastes and simmer for 5 minutes, stirring occasionally. Make sure that the pastes do not burn as it will turn bitter.

Mix in the pork ribs and stir fry for about 5 minutes, ensuring the meat is coated in the sauce. Then pour in the water and simmer for about 30 minutes. You can choose to cover the wok but do keep an eye on the water level if you do so. Stir occasionally. Keep the fire low. If you see the dish drying up, add some more water to prevent the bottom from burning. Cook till tender yet retaining a good bite.

Towards the end of the cooking, taste the sauce and make adjustments if needed, adding soy sauce or sugar.

Before you dish out, add the spring onions, stir, and switch off the fire. Garnish with coriander leaves and diced chillies just before you serve.

TOW YEW BAK
Braised Belly Pork in Soy Sauce

What the Hokkiens call Tau Yew Bak is a staple and comfort food for many Chinese households in Southeast Asia.

My Mum's version is dry, garlicky and made with the dark, thick caramelized soy sauce commonly found in Malaysia. It is perfect with a bowl of rice and Sambal Belacan. She often added hard-boiled eggs and *tau korn* (firm beancurd).

The key to good Tau Yew Bak is to cook it "slow and low". The meat should not be falling apart but yet tender enough to cut through easily with a fork.

Use a good-quality pot, with thicker material and good heat distribution to avoid bottom burning. It should also be wide enough to ensure even cooking.

As this is a soy sauce-based dish, you should use good quality sauces. Superior light soy sauce is tastier and less salty. If you cannot get the variety of thick and dark soy sauce which is dense in its viscosity, other types of dark sauce can be used.

The pork belly cut is perfect for this dish but add some shoulder pork if you want leaner meat too. Leave some of the garlic whole if you enjoy them that way. Dried Chinese mushrooms can be added but note that the taste of the dish will change considerably. Chestnuts will sweeten the sauce.

Use the timing given in the recipe as a guide since the size of the pieces of pork, the thickness and material of the pot, and the heat are variables which affect timing. You do not need to add any cooking oil if you are using the pork belly cut.

Tow Yew Bak

1 kg (2.2 lb) pork belly
10 cloves garlic
10 pieces rock sugar or
  5 tsps sugar
2 star anise
15 white peppercorns, crushed
1 cinnamon stick
2 tbsps dark soy sauce
4 tbsps light soy sauce
4 hard boiled eggs
1 sprig coriander leaves

Slice the pork belly, skin on, into 2-cm (0.8-in) cubes. Give the garlic a gentle whack with a cleaver to expose some of the flesh.

Heat up a pot over a low flame. Add the rock sugar and let it melt and caramelize. Add the star anise, peppercorn, cinnamon stick and garlic. There will be some popping. Watch out for it.

Put in the pork and stir. After 5 minutes, add the dark and light soy sauces. Stir, mix and cover the pot. Let it braise gently over low fire for 40 minutes. Remember to turn the pork occasionally to ensure that there is no bottom burning.

Hard boil the eggs in a separate pot of water and peel off the shells. Add to the pot after the meat has cooked for about 30 minutes. If you are using firm soy bean cakes, you can also add them at this point.

If you need more sauce, add some water towards the end of cooking time. However, I do not like watery versions of Tau Yew Bak and prefer the sauce to be more intense.

Served warm, garnished with coriander leaves.

BRAISED PORK KNUCKLES

Slow poached *yin tai* (Cantonese for Braised Pork Knuckles) was a regular feature at our Chinese New Year reunion dinners. Unlike the German Roasted Pork Knuckles, where the skin needs to be crackly and crispy, this Chinese version goes the opposite direction. The skin and fat need to be soft, creamy and yet firm enough to be picked up with a pair of chopsticks.

If you are trying to diet (and that is a forbidden word during Chinese New Year), knuckles done this way will literally bring you to your knees. It is spectacular as the skin and fat are the first things you see. In fact, cooked and presented correctly, it should be the only thing you see at first. And when it is placed on the table, the whole thing shimmers. No kidding. Like the shimmering glass of water on the car's dashboard as the dinosaur approaches in the movie Jurassic Park, it will make for a spectacular effect. If you look carefully, you can also see an image of yourself after the shimmering stops. You dig in with your chopsticks, shattering your portrait. You let it melt in your mouth. The flavour and texture hits you as the unmentionable swirls in your chops – rich, creamy, fruity, spicy and aromatically complex. Swine can be better than wine, as they say.

The key is to braise it very slowly on low fire. As the knuckle is a special cut, you may have to order it ahead from your butcher.

1 pork knuckle, skin on	Deep fry or scald the knuckle in hot water. This will firm up the skin and keep it from tearing as you braise.
6 dried shitake mushrooms, rehydrated, stems removed	
2 tbsps rock sugar	Heat up the oil in a deep wok or pot.
3 slices ginger	
3 cloves garlic	Add the rock sugar and simmer over low heat till it melts
2 cinnamon sticks	
2 star anise	Add the ginger, garlic and spices and stir fry for 2 minutes. Add the pork knuckle and the rest of the seasoning and the red yeast if you are using it. Pour in the water to cover the knuckle. Include the mushrooms.
1 liquorice stick (*gam cho*)	
10 white peppercorns	
2 cardamons	
1 black cardamon (optional)	
240 ml (1 cup) light soy sauce	Simmer for 3 hours or till it is soft enough. A fork should go into the fat eaily if the meat is cooked.
1 tbsp dark soy sauce	
2 tbsps Chinese rice wine	
1 tsp red glutinous yeast for colouring (optional)	Add the cornstarch slurry to thicken the sauce.
240 ml (1 cup) water	Adjust the taste with salt or sugar if needed.
2 tsps cornflour made into a slurry with 2 tbsps water	
Salt and sugar to taste	Place the pork on some lettuce leaves and garnish with coriander leaves. Serve it hot with chili sauce on the side.
Butter lettuce leaves	
Coriander leaves	
2 tbsp oil	

GOING SLOW AND LOW

FOOD TEXTURE IS IMPORTANT in most Asian cuisines. So use the right cooking technique for different cuts of meat to get the optimum texture for a particular dish.

I came across an interesting poem by Su Shi, a poet, painter, calligrapher, pharmacologist, gastronome, and statesman of the Song dynasty. Su Shi, also known as Su Dongpo, was apparently the creator of Dong Po Pork, the famous dish of braised belly pork from Hangzhou.

He wrote this poem entitled "Eating Pork":

慢着火、少着水
柴火罨焰烟不起
待它自熟莫催它
火候足时它自美

Low-temperature, less water
Small flames, a little smoke
Let it cook and never hasten
The right heat gives a natural taste

Note the advice of this sage: "Let it cook and never hasten."

If you use high heat on meat in the hope that the cooking process can be shortened, the meat will shrink, harden and lose most of its flavours. This is true especially for tougher cuts like pork ribs and pork belly which typically need longer cooking time.

If you braise meat gently or go "slow and low", you will achieve an optimum balance of flavour and texture. You are aiming to achieve what is known as *song hau* in Cantonese – a texture with toothsome succulence. You do not want the meat to be falling apart like American pulled pork.

Many cooking techniques, such as steaming, braising over low fire, double boiling and even setting modern ovens to low, observe this "slow and low" principle. *Sous vide* cooking is one easy way of cooking with precise control of temperature.

This "slow and low" approach is useful when cooking Tow Yew Bak (page 65), various pork rib recipes, Beef Rendang (page 87) and Braised Pork Knuckles (page 67). The lower temperature ensures the fat, key to the texture of these dishes, is not melted away.

Understanding and being patient with your cooking will help you to get better results.

As it is said in Proverbs 16:32:

Better a patient person than a warrior,
one with self-control than one who takes a city.

Don't rush your meat dishes.

STIR FRIED ROAST PORK

This was the first dish I learnt to cook.

As a young boy, I helped out in my Mum's canteen. Her customers requested for her Siew Yoke (roast pork) to be fried in sauce.

I can recall that the wok looked really huge. I was blessed with some height even at that age and that helped. My mum had taught me to add some oil, garlic, sugar and dark sauce. In a huge hot wok, a small plate of Siew Yoke turned out really nice cooked this way. It was also good wok practice for me.

If you have leftover roast pork, this is a delicious dish to cook. It is easy. After all, a 7-year-old child made this! The sugar and dark soy sauce will caramelize the Siew Yoke nicely. The key is to cook with enough heat and long enough to crisp and caramelize the skin of the roast pork, garlic and ginger bits. It is fantastic eaten with rice.

300 g (10.5 oz) sliced roast pork
  (Siu Yoke)
1 tbsp oil
1 tbsp minced ginger
1 tbsp minced garlic
1 tsp dark soy sauce
1 tsp soy sauce
1 tsp sugar
Dash of white pepper
Coriander leaves as garnish

Heat up a wok over medium fire. Add the oil and, when it is hot, fry the ginger for a minute before adding the garlic and roast pork. Continue frying.

Add the sauces, white pepper and sugar. Continue to stir-fry till the meat is caramelized and the skin is crispy.

Dish out, garnish with coriander leaves, and serve immediately.

WOK-COOKED CHAR SIEW

This Cantonese roasted sweet pork (Char Siew) is universally loved. My Mum's Char Siew recipe is very popular and many have used it successfully. It uses a simple list of ingredients and a convenient method of cooking that is suited for the home kitchen.

Traditionally, Char Siew is skewered and cooked in a charcoal roaster. The word *char* means 'skewer' and *siew*, 'roasting'. It has a sticky, caramelized reddish appearance and the taste is sweet. Outside the Cantonese world, Char Siew, without a proper English-translated name, is often confused with the more savoury Siew Yoke or Roasted Pork Belly which comes with a cracking skin, another popular Cantonese dish which can be cooked in the same roaster.

A good Char Siew should have these qualities:

The exterior should be caramelized, glazed and sticky with some parts charred. When hung and cooked in a traditional charcoal roaster, the uneven surface of the pork strips from a well-marbled butt or shoulder cut has bits and corners which are charred as the heat from the roaster is concentrated on these parts. The soy-based marinade gives the attractive reddish appearance, although the hue is sometimes enhanced by adding red yeast or artificial colouring.

As for the texture, a properly done Char Siew has a good bite (*song hau*) and should be succulent, moist and juicy, not dry or overcooked. The meat should not break apart like American pulled pork.

Needless to say, the best way to cook Char Siew is to use a traditional meat roaster in which strips of pork are hung and roasted in high heat. The roaster makes it easier for basting, the constant process which helps to impart a caramelized surface, adds flavours and also moderates the heat, ensuring that the pork is not over-charred on the exterior before the meat is cooked through. The pork is also cooked in its own juices, with the sugars left behind as the moisture drips down the meat and evaporates in the high heat. This high heat and the presence of sugars result in complex Mallard reactions on the meat, enhancing the flavours further, like the way pan-searing or grilling a steak will.

In the home kitchen, the oven is normally used. However, my Mum used the wok to cook it because the method is quick and convenient. From start to finish, it takes less than an hour and you are using only the wok. There is no need to marinade the meat beforehand and you end up with a nice sauce as a by-product.

She started by braising the pork belly strips in the sauce, simmering slowly, till the meat became tender in the thickening sauce. Then she increased the fire slightly so that the meat would be charred in parts in the caramelized sauce. Sometimes, she also removed some of the sauce and increased the heat to sear the meat. She used a metal wok – stainless steel, carbonized steel or cast iron – as it is an effective conductor of heat for the searing phase. A non-stick wok will not do as the non-stick material will flake off in the high heat required.

Stubborn stains will be left behind from the searing. To clean the wok, just heat up some water in it and scrape off the stains with a stiff spatula.

Mum normally marinated the pork for about an hour before cooking it, especially if leaner cuts were used. But if she was short of time, she knew that the cooking process would flavour the fatty pork well, even without marination.

The choice cut of pork for this wok method is skinless pork belly. Apart from the fact that some pork fat is always delicious, the layers of fat ensures that there is a larger window for optimal cooking so that the meat is not overcooked but remains juicy.

That said, if you prefer shoulder, armpit or butt, use them. Pork jowl is good too. The Char Siew you get from these cuts is different as they do not have the fatty layers. But, done properly, they can be very nice, with a succulent bite.

If you are using these cuts, I recommend that you marinate them for a few hours. You do this not just to add flavours but also to introduce liquid into the lean pork. This way, the meat will be more succulent and will not dry up so much. Properly speaking, you are brining the meat. I also recommend that you add a bit more oil.

The thickness of the strips, the heat and type of wok or pan used will have a bearing on cooking time. The rectangular cross-section of the pork strips should be about 2 x 3 cm (0.8 x 1.2 in).

My mum added some bicarbonate of soda to tenderize the meat when marinating it. This step is optional but it does cut down the cooking time.

Flavour-wise, what you put into the meat is what you get since there is very little loss of flavours when using the wok method. So, do taste the marinade before adding it to the meat. If you use cheap salt (my recipe calls for table salt), your meat will turn out too salty.

Note that the wok method does not work very well for batches of meat that are 3 kilograms (6.6 lbs) and above, because stacking the meat will mean uneven cooking. Some use a two-step wok cum oven method which works too.

Char Siew, accompanied by sliced fresh cucumbers, is delicious with sauce poured over steaming rice. Some Malaysian wonton noodles are served with Char Siew sauce. Leftover Char Siew has many uses, including Fried Rice and, in a bun to make Char Siew Pao.

Master this simple recipe and it will quickly become a go-to dinner dish – and your family will thank you for it.

Wok-Cooked Char Siew

1 kg (2.2 lb) pork belly
2 tbsps oil
240 ml (1 cup) water

Marinade
2 tsps table salt
1 tsp sesame oil
1 tsp thick dark soy sauce
1 tsp white pepper
1 tsp five-spice powder
1 tbsp sugar
2 tsps *hoi sin* sauce
2 tbsps honey
1 tbsp Chinese wine or
   1 tsp brandy

Cut the belly pork into strips of about 2 x 3 cm (0.8 x 1.2 in) in rectangular cross section. Remove the skin but leave the fat.

Mix the marinade and soak the strips of pork in it.

Heat up the wok with the oil. Place the pork strips in one layer in the wok, then put in the rest of the marinade and the water.

Gently braise it over a small fire. Turn the strips from time to time. You don't need to cover the wok if you are monitoring the level of the liquid. If the liquid evaporates too quickly, add some water.

After about 40 minutes, the meat should be tender. A fork should go into the meat easily but it should not fall apart.

By now, the sauce would have thickened. Remove most of the sauce. Increase to medium fire and sear the strips of meat. In the main, you want to cause Mallard reactions and introduce some searing, similar to the way you sear a steak.

Brush some of the sauce and extra honey on the meat and let it rest till it reaches room temperature before slicing and serving.

Serve the extra sauce as a gravy.

ZHAR YOKE
Hakka Deep-Fried Pork

This irresistible snack – Hakka Deep-Fried Pork or Zhar Yoke – is one of my Mum's signature dishes which I eventually managed to replicate.

I said "eventually" because I could not get it right, even though I followed her written recipe. Or so I thought. I was using *fu yee* (white fermented bean curd) and it was only on the eighth try when I realised that I should have been using *nam yee* (red fermented beancurd) as written in her recipe.

Zhar Yoke is a delightful snack which can be eaten on its own – and it will be hard to stop once you start – or served with rice. It can also be cooked further with wood ear fungus, where it then becomes the popular dish called Hakka Braised Pork Belly.

As the skin can be difficult to crisp up, you can choose to remove it.

1 kg (2.2 lb) pork belly
  (*sam chan yoke*)

Marinade
3 pieces red fermented bean
  curd (*nam yee*)
1 tsp five-spice powder
½ tsp salt
1 tbsp sugar
½ tbsp sesame oil
2 tbsps chopped garlic
½ tsp thick dark soy source
1 egg
½ tsp white pepper
2 tbsps Chinese rice wine or
  1 tbsp brandy

Flour mixture
2 tbsps plain flour
1 tbsp rice flour
1 tbsp cornflour

Oil for deep frying

Remove the skin of the pork. Cut the pork into 2½-cm (1-in) cubes.

Mix all ingredients for the marinade and marinate the pork for at least 4 hours or overnight.

Heat oil in wok for deep frying.

Combine the 3 types of flour for the flour mixture.

Dip the pieces of pork into the flour to coat them very lightly. The purpose of the flour is to create a thin layer of batter to hold the seasoning. The result after deep frying should *not* be a layer of crispy batter.

Deep fry the pieces of pork till they are brown.

HAKKA BRAISED PORK BELLY

This is how to make Hakka Braised Pork Belly from Hakka Zhar Yoke.

1 portion Hakka Zhar Yoke
  (page 79)
100 g wood ear fungus
1 tbsp Chinese wine

Sauce
2 pieces red fermented beancurd
  (*nam yee*)
400 ml (1.7 cups) water

Dissolve the fermented bean curd in the water to make a sauce.

In a pot, combine the sauce, black fungus, Chinese wine and the fried pork and stir. Partially cover the pot and slowly braise for 1 hour or till the meat and skin are soft and tender.

Serve it warm. Best eaten with rice.

BAKWAN KEPITING
Nonya Pork and Crab Meatball Soup

My mother made many dear friends when she spent her last 15 years in Singapore. One of them is Lucy Kwok who loved her dearly.

Lucy has become a very close family friend and she is also my regular cooking mate. She also plays a major role in the Food Ministry at St James' Church. Her love for food, cooking and generous spirit is an inspiration to many.

I am glad that I can feature one of her signature recipes, the Nonya classic Bakwan Kepiting, in this cookbook. This soup is a favorite during festive occasions and is best savoured as a starter.

For this recipe, make sure you get fresh flower crabs. Forget about frozen crab meat. These crabs are great for seafood stock as they are sweet. Taking out the meat needs some effort but, as the shells are soft, it is not difficult to do that. Using lean pork will keep the oil to a minimum, making a clear soup.

The winter bamboo shoot adds a crunchy texture. Lucy uses the ready-cooked ones from the supermarket. Don't forget the roasted garlic. Bakwan Kepiting is not the same without it.

4 large flower crabs
600 g (1.3 lb) minced lean pork
3 chicken carcasses
1 large yellow onion
6 litres (1.5 gal) water

500 g (1.1 lb) winter bamboo
  shoot, cut into strips
1 tsp chicken granules
1 tbsp sesame oil
4 tbsps light soya sauce
1 tsp salt or to taste
White pepper to taste
2 tbsps cornflour

Garnishing
Coriander leaves, chopped
  roughly
12 cloves garlic, finely diced and
  roasted to golden brown,
  drained
White pepper to taste

Heat up a dry wok. Put the crabs in and cover the wok and cook for 8 minutes. You are effectively using the wok as an oven. This method is convenient as the crab is kept dry, which makes separating the meat easier. Shell the crabs, set aside crab meat, and keep the shells for the stock.

To prepare the stock, simmer the chicken carcasses and the crab shells with one yellow onion in 6 litres (1.5 gal) for 45 minutes. Strain.

Mix the minced pork with the crab meat. Add half the bamboo strips in, chicken granules, sesame oil, light soy sauce, salt, pepper and cornflour. Mix well and make a ball of about 2½ cm (1 in) in diameter. Cook it and taste for texture and flavour and adjust, if required, to your taste. When you are satisfied, make the meat balls.

Bring the stock to the boil and add in the remaining bamboo shoots and the meat balls. The meat balls will float when they are cooked. Remove immediatiely and set aside. You do not want them to be overcooked.

To serve, put 2 or 3 meat balls in a soup bowl. Add some soup and strips of bamboo shoot. Garnish with fried garlic, coriander leaves, and add a dash of white pepper.

DRY INDIAN LAMB CURRY

I love dry lamb curry and mutton curry. It is a perfect match for Roti Prata. Cut bite-sized, you can wrap the *roti* around it. If the meat is just right (not overly soft) and the curry is infused with spices and the glorious flavour of lamb or mutton, every bite will make you bleat with pleasure.

As lamb is a strong-tasting meat, you should use some strong spices and herbs to cook it. Ginger will work well. If you are using mutton, which is tougher, you will have to cook it longer. As always, the timing in the recipe is just a guide and you should be free to take bites along the way to both test and enjoy your curry.

Serve it warm. It is also great with basmati rice, cucumber *raita* or just plain yoghurt.

Here's my Mum's take on mutton curry.

2 kg (4.4 lb) lamb, shoulder or leg	Cut the meat into 2½-cm (1-in) cubes.
1 tsp coriander seeds ½ tsp cumin seeds ½ tsp fennel seeds	Toast the coriander seeds, cumin seeds, and fennel seeds and blend finely.
12 cloves garlic, skinned 30 g (1 oz) shallots or 7 medium Bombay onions, skinned	Blend the garlic, onions and ginger into a paste.
2 tbsps diced ginger 2 star anise 2 tbsps oil or ghee	Heat up 2 tablespoons of oil or ghee in a pot or wok. Add the paste, blended spices and star anise. Include 1 teaspoon each of salt and sugar.
30 dried chillies, blended into a paste or 200 g (7 oz) chilli paste 25 g (1 cup) curry leaves Salt	Add some chilli paste. Indian curries need some "kick" and you should not be afraid to add more at this stage. The heat depends on what type of dried chillies you are using.
Sugar 1 kg (2.2 lbs) yellow potatoes, peeled	Simmer for about 20 minutes, adding some water if the mixture is too dry.
Yoghurt to taste	Put in the curry leaves and lamb. Add 200 ml (0.8 cup) of water and simmer, keeping the fire low for 45 minutes or more, tasting along the way and adjusting with salt or sugar to get the flavour balance and texture according to your taste. If you are adding peeled yellow potatoes, do it mid way of this step.
	Add some yoghurt to the curry. This adds some sourness and creaminess. More or less is up to you.
	You will know the meat is cooked when you can cut through it easily with a spoon. But the meat should not be falling apart.

BEEF RENDANG

The Nonya and Malay roots of my Mum's cooking comes to the fore in one of her favourite curry dishes: Beef Rendang.

Slowly braising tough cuts of beef in curry, Beef Rendang is to Malays and Indonesians what Beef Bourguignon is to the French.

According to tradition, it is an Indonesian dish. As the meat is cooked for a long time (*merandang* in Indonesian) till the curry is dried out, it can keep well. This explains why the recipe was popular during pre-refrigeration times. There are two types of *rendang*, the dry and wet varieties. The dry one can keep very well, even in room temperature. In fact, dry Beef Rendang is almost like beef jerky.

Amongst curries, *rendang* takes the longest to cook. Depending on the cut used, the size of the portions, and quantity, it can go up to two hours or more. Strong herbs like kaffir lime leaves (*daun limau perut*) and blue ginger (*lengkuas*, galangal) are added.

For my Mum, the use of Kerisik (page 237) makes *rendang*, *rendang*. *Kerisik* is a Malay word and if there is to be an English translation, it has to be this: grated coconut toasted and pounded into oily submission. To achieve this, the grated coconut is slowly toasted in a wok till it is golden, then pounded in a mortar till it turns into an oily, glistening paste.

I can see and smell the Kerisik as I write this. For when it comes to mortar work, it is where I usually step in. Being the youngest in the Wong family, I was the lowest in the food chain. And so, I had to lower myself, squat and pound away. It was rather therapeutic to see the toasted loose bits of grated coconut transform into a smooth, glistening, gluey and oily paste. It gets increasingly hard to pound because the coconut will cause the pestle to stick to the mortar. This is how I know the metamorphosis is taking place. The result, with its unforgettable fragrance, is the heart of a *rendang*.

You can still make an acceptable version of Kerisik by toasting the grated coconut and grinding it in an electric chopper till the oily paste is achieved. You do not need a large quantity. Two to three tablespoons of Kerisik will be sufficient for 2-3 kg (4.4-6.6 lbs) of beef. However, it is convenient to make a large batch and freeze what is not used. It keeps well for months.

As for the cut of beef, shin beef is popular. It does not take as long to cook as other cuts like topside. However, I prefer the latter as the meat will turn out firmer but flakes easily in strings, as good Beef Rendang should.

Beef Rendang

2 kg (4.4 lb) topside, cut into
  4 cm (1½ in) cubes
1 fresh coconut, grated without
  any husk

Spice paste
30 dried chillies
20 shallots
2½ cm (1 in) turmeric (*kunyit*)
5 cm (2 in) blue ginger (*lengkuas,*
  galangal), thinly sliced
5 cm (2 in) ginger, thinly sliced
½ tsp cumin seeds
1 tsp coriander seeds
240 ml (1 cup) cooking oil
200 ml (⁴/₅ cup) coconut cream

Gula melaka (palm sugar) or
  white sugar
2 pieces dried *Garcinia*
  Cambogia fruit (*assam keping*)
1 cinnamon stick, 5-8 cm (2-3 in)
3 star anise
5 cardamom pods
5 cloves
2 tbsps salt
2 lemongrass bulbs
5 kaffir lime leaves (*daun limau*
  perut), stems removed and the
  leaf blades sliced finely

Making the Kerisik

In a wok on low fire, toast the grated coconut till it is golden brown, but not burnt. Stir constantly. It will take about 30 minutes. Using a mortar and pestle, pound the toasted coconut in small batches till it is an oily and sticky paste.

If you squeezed the grated coconut to extract the milk, it will be harder to produce an oily Kerisik. So, leave the milk in. One grated coconut can produce a bowl of Kerisik. Store the bulk in the freezer for future use.

Preparing the beef

Cut the beef into 4 cm (1½ in) cubes. The beef will shrink as you braise. You can choose to have larger pieces. Just ensure that the cubes are of the same size for uniform cooking. Larger pieces will need longer cooking time.

Preparing the paste

Soak the dried chillies. Peel the onions, turmeric, blue ginger and ginger, and slice into small pieces.

Toast the cumin seeds and coriander seeds together for a minute in a dry wok.

Blend these prepared spices together coarsely to make a spice paste.

Cooking the *rendang*

Bruise the white lemongrass bulbs – just give it good whacks with the blunt side of a chopper.

Heat up the oil in a wok. Put in the spice paste, half of the Kerisik, cinnamon stick, star anise, cardamom pods, cloves, *assam keping* and salt. Simmer over low fire for 15 minutes.

Slide in the beef cubes and mix into the paste.

Add the coconut cream and enough water till it just covers the meat. Put in the lemongrass bulbs.

Simmer over low heat for about 2 hours in or till the meat

is tender. Stir occasionally. If the curry dries up too quickly, add some water to prevent the bottom from burning. Burning your *rendang* is bad. The burnt taste will permeate the whole dish and it cannot be rescued. Using a good wok or pot with a thick bottom will lessen the chances of burning.

Stir in the rest of the Kerisik and sprinkle on the sliced kaffir lime leaves just before serving.

You can serve Beef Rendang warm or at room temperature. It goes very well with rice, bread, Ketupat (steamed rice cakes) or Lemang (steamed glutinous rice cakes).

Note: If you use beef shin, it can cut down the cooking time by half. Chicken Rendang tastes *sedap* (delicious) too. The cooking time is shorter and the chicken is cut into large serving pieces.

SEAFOOD

HAR LOK
Fried River Prawns in Soy Bean Sauce

The best prawns I have ever eaten are the fresh river prawns caught wild from the rivers of Malaysia.

They are always eaten whole, with the shells and head on. The flesh is succulent and sweet, with a muscular texture which lends a crunchy bite. The head is usually full of the goodness of the roe.

One favorite recipe for prawns is Har Lok which uses dried and preserved soy beans, ginger and garlic. The whole prawns are first coated lightly in flour and deep fried. Then the sauce is prepared and the prawns are coated with it.

It is a must-have dish on my Chinese New Year reunion dinner table. I can still recall once when my brother in Ipoh managed to lay his hands on some large, fresh, wild-caught prawns. They were swimming in the tank when he bought them. Mum cooked them the Har Lok way and sliced each into half, lengthwise. With a small teaspoon in hand, we dug into the head first. It was an exquisite experience and remain an important memory of my Mum's cooking and her love she showed to us through it.

It is harder these days to find wild-caught prawns and we have to be content with farmed ones. This recipe is delicious too with large sea prawns.

Har Lok

1 kg (2.2 lb) river prawns
Oil for deep frying
2 tbsps cornflour
240 ml (1 cup) water
Coriander leaves

Sauce
2 tbsps finely diced young ginger
1 tbsp chopped garlic
1 tbsp sugar
1 tbsp dark soy bean paste
   (*tau see*)
2 tbsps light soy bean paste
   (*tau cheong*)
1 tbsp light soy sauce
1 tsp dark soy sauce
3 red chilies, diced
3 stalks spring onions, cut into
   2½-cm (1-in) strips
2 tbsps Chinese wine

Clean up the prawns by first giving them a hair cut. Use scissors to snip off the all the hairy stuff that is sticking out, the pointy horn at the head and pedicure the frilly legs. You may have to dig out with a toothpick the lump of sand or debris in the heads at the spot where you have snipped off the horn.

Coat the prawns lightly with the cornflour.

Deep fry the prawns in hot oil for 3-4 minutes. The prawns will turn into a beautiful golden color when cooked. Remove the prawns and set aside.

Heat up 3 tablespoons of the leftover oil in the wok over a small fire. Put in the chopped ginger first and, after a minute, add garlic, sugar, the dark and light soy bean sauces and chillies. Stir fry briefly until fragrant but do not burn the sauce. Sprinkle some water in if the sauce is sticking to the wok or burning up.

Add the prawns and stir fry for about 2 minutes to mix with the sauce.

Mix a tablespoon of cornflour in a cup of water. Then add it to the prawns and stir fry. Immediately, add the spring onions and wine. Stir fry for half a minute and the dish is ready to be served.

Garnish with coriander leaves. Best eaten with rice.

FRIED ASSAM PRAWNS

Fried prawns marinated in *assam* or tamarind sauce is a Nonya delicacy. It is one of our Wong family favorites, whether eaten with rice or as a snack by itself. It is also a fabulous accompaniment for Nasi Lemak (see page 179).

The prawns are marinated in tamarind paste, sugar, salt and thick dark soy sauce. It is then patiently pan seared in a shallow layer of oil. The prawns are served whole with shells and heads on.

The key to good Fried Assam Prawns lies in the way you cook it. It is easier to just deep fry, especially when cooking large batches. While your prawns will look better, most of the marinade will dissipate. When you pan sear or shallow pan fry, the marinated prawns will have direct contact with the pan's hot surface so as to effectively caramelize the sauce on the shells and to get them charred and sticky. This add layers of flavours – salty, sour, sweet and umami.

Now, this approach is labor-intensive as you can only pan sear a few prawns at one go, being limited by the size of the pan. This is one reason why, commercially, it is seldom cooked this way.

If done properly, the prawns will be covered by black blotches. It will be lacking in visual appeal but the taste, stickiness and texture is unique. The uglier it looks, the better the taste!

To enjoy these prawns, you should eat everything. It is shell-crunching time. This is one reason why crystal prawns with their thinner shells are more suited for this recipe than tiger prawns.

For your comfort, I have given measurements. But this is one dish which you should try making according to your taste buds and learn to adjust along the way. The dark soy sauce adds to the caramelization when you fry the prawns.

Fried Assam Prawns

1 kg (2.2 lb) medium-sized
   crystal prawns
200 g (7 oz) tamarind pulp
2 tsps sugar
2 tsps salt
1 tsp white pepper
2 tsps thick dark soy sauce
Calamansi limes

Soak the tamarind pulp in a cup of hot water. Then press with your fingers to loosen and dissolve the pulp to make a paste. You do not need to remove the seeds.

Next, marinate the prawns with the tamarind paste, sugar, salt, pepper and dark soya sauce for 30 minutes.

Use the largest flat pan you have. Heat up a shallow layer of oil (about 1 mm) in the pan.

Put in some prawns, few enough so that you don't need to stack them up. You should hear some sizzling when you put the prawns in. Use medium flame but control it, alternating between low to medium to crisp the exterior while keeping the meat moist. The prawns need to look burnt in parts, caramelized and aromatic. Press the prawns lightly to increase surface contact with the pan.

You may have to refresh and clean the pan after two or three batches.

When the prawns are cooked, put them in a colander or on top of paper towels so that the oil can be drained.

Drizzle some lime juice on before you serve. The prawns can be eaten warm or at room temperature. In fact, they taste even better the day after.

SAMBAL UDANG
Prawn Sambal

Prawn Sambal was another dish my Mum made regularly. Served with a plate of rice and cold cucumber with some mint leaves, it is a meal on its own. Her version is drier than most and she had only one secret – if you can call it such – the blended lemongrass.

Use fresh prawns. The prawns need to be cooked quickly. If you cook it too slowly (i.e. with oil that is not hot enough or by overcrowding), the meat will not be firm. So, make sure that the sambal you have cooked is hot before you add prawns to it.

If you are cooking a large portion, I will recommend two-stage frying. Use some heated oil to quickly cook small batches of the peeled prawns. Then you use the same oil to fry the sambal before coating the cooked prawns with it. The recipe below uses this approach.

1 kg (2.2 lb) prawns
3 lemongrass bulbs
10 shallots
5 dried red chillies
5 fresh red chillies
1 tbsp shrimp paste (*belacan*)
200 ml (0.8 cup) oil
5 kaffir lime leaves (*daun limau perut*), diced finely
240 ml (1 cup) water
Salt to taste
Sugar to taste
Cornflour

2 cucumbers, sliced
A bunch of mint leaves
Wedges of lime

Peel the prawns. Marinate the prawn meat with 1 teaspoon each of salt and sugar before dusting with the cornflour. Refrigerate for 30 minutes.

Meanwhile, you prepare the sambal. Dice up the lemongrass bulbs. Blend the shallots and lemongrass finely. Soak the dried chillies in hot water for 10 minutes. Remove and blend along with the fresh chillies. Toast the piece of *belacan* in a dry pan or wok over low fire for a minute. Set aside.

Remove the prawns from the fridge and rinse off the cornflour and shake off excess water.

Heat up the 200 ml of oil in a wok. Fry the prawns in small batches till they are golden orange. Set aside.

Add the chilli paste, *belacan* and the lemongrass-shallot paste to the leftover oil and simmer for 15 minutes. Add the water. Season with salt and sugar to taste.

Put the prawns in with the finely diced kaffir lime leaves and stir fry for 1 minute.

Serve with sliced cucumber, mint leaves and halved limes. Squeeze on the lime juice at the dinner table to maximize the fresh tang. This dish can be served at room temperature and enjoyed eaten with hands in the traditional Asian way.

UDANG NENAS
Prawn and Pineapple Sambal or Curry

Udang Nenas is a popular Nonya and Malay recipe. In these cuisines, pineapple is commonly used in savory dishes as an appetizer or as a main. My Mum sometimes made this dish to go with Nasi Lemak (page 201).

Use unripe pineapples. Braising them slowly in a sweet curry so that the flavours meld will give you delicious and crunchy pineapple pieces and an an appetising pineapple-flavoured curry.

1 small pineapple or half a large
   pineapple
5 cloves garlic, sliced lengthwise
1 kg (2.2 lb) large prawns,
   trimmed and shelled, if
   preferrred
1 tsp shrimp paste (*belacan*)
100 ml (0.4 cup) cooking oil
1 tsp salt
1 tsp sugar
100 ml (0.4 cup) water

Spice paste
10 small onions
2 tsps chopped blue ginger
   (*lengkuas*, galangal)
3 lemongrass bulbs
3 candlenuts (*buah keras*)
10 dried chillies or a mixture
   of fresh chillies and bird's eye
   chillies

Garnish
Coriander leaves

Slice the pineapples into 1-cm (0.4-in) thick rings and cut each ring into half. Clean up the prawns but leave the shells on.

Pound or blend together the spice paste ingredients.

Toast the *belacan* in a dry pan or wok.

Heat up the oil. Put in the blended ingredients and stir-fry and simmer over a gentle flame for about 10 minutes.

Add the pineapples and stir-fry for a minute. Season with salt and sugar.

Pour in the water and simmer for another 10 minues or till the pineapple is translucent. Taste and adjust the seasoning to your liking.

Increase the fire and add the prawns. Stir-fry briefly and cover the wok for 3 minutes.

Garnish with coriander leaves and serve warm with rice.

SANTAN PRAWNS
Prawns in Coconut Milk

This is a dish Mum made regularly. She simply called it Santan Prawns, *santan* being coconut milk. As I have not encountered this dish outside our home, I am not sure what the real name is or whether it was my Mum who concocted this recipe. In any case, it has obvious Thai-Northern and Malay influence and is somewhat similar to Tom Yum Soup.

Is it a soup or a curry? It leans more to the former. Diners should have a separate bowl to scoop it into and drink from there.

Leave the heads and shells on the prawns. If you have to peel them, just remove the shells from the body for easier eating. The flavours from the inside of the head are important for this curry. Kaffir lime leaves and blue ginger contribute scent and flavour to the soup. Don't boil them for too long or it will impart a bitter tinge.

It's better to use a claypot for this dish so that you can keep the soup heated for dinner and serve it straight from the stove to the table. It's an easy dish to prepare and fast to cook.

600 g (1.3 lb) large prawns
2 tbsps oil
10 shallots, sliced
10 cloves garlic, sliced
1 tsp shrimp paste (*belacan*)
2 tsps chilli paste
1 tsp salt
400 ml (1.7 cup) water
100 ml (0.4 cup) coconut milk
3 lemongrass bulbs, smashed
2½ cm (1 in) turmeric (*kunyit*),
    finely sliced
2½ cm (1 in) blue ginger
    (galangal, *lengkuas*), sliced
4 kaffir lime leaves
    (*daun limau perut*)
2 green chillies, each sliced each
    into 3 pieces
Coriander leaves
	Heat the oil in a small pot or claypot.
	
	Add the slices of shallots and garlic. Add *belacan*, chilli paste and salt. Stir for about 2 minutes till fragrant.
	
	Pour in the water and coconut milk. Gently heat it up and then add the rest of the herbs.
	
	Include the prawns. Cover the pot and switch off the fire. The prawns should be cooked through after 5 minutes. Garnish with coriander leaves and serve immediately. Best eaten with rice.

GLASS VERMICELLI PRAWNS

This is another signature prawn noodle recipe which I have learned from Mrs Lucy Kwok.

This recipe showcases *tung fun*, fine glass vermicelli which is made from mung bean starch. Like *mai fun* (rice vermicelli), *tung fun* absorbs flavours very well and is often cooked with seafood like prawns and crabs. Sometimes it is added to vegetarian dishes like Chai Choi (page 131) or Sayur Lodeh.

Glass Vermicelli Prawns was one of the hawker dishes which I used to enjoy very much. For some reason, it is hardly sold these days. So, I was delighted to come across it again when Lucy Kwok cooked it for a party.

The firm tiger prawns or any fresh sea prawns will be best for this dish. It is best to leave the heads and shells on for this recipe. The prawn-flavoured and smooth *tung fun* is a joy to eat.

While Lucy's version does not use eggs, I do prefer to scramble some eggs into the noodles as they absorb the flavours well too, adding another dimension to the dish.

600 g (1.3 lb) medium-sized
  prawns
480 ml (2 cups) chicken stock
400 g (14 oz) glass vermicelli
  (*tung fun*)
200 g (7 oz) Chinese cabbage
  (*wong bok*)
6 cloves garlic
2 stalks coriander, chopped finely
  root reserved
150 g (5 oz) bean sprouts
240 ml (1 cup) oil

For the sauce
3 tbsps fish sauce
3 tbsps light soya sauce
2 tbsps dark soy sauce
2 tbsps sesame oil
1 chicken stock cube

For garnishing
Coriander leaves
Fried shallots

Soak the glass vermicelli in cold water for about 10 minutes. Slice the cabbage into bite-sized pieces. Slice the garlic into flakes.

Heat up the oil in a wok and fry the prawns till they turn golden red. Sprinkle fish sauce to your taste over them and transfer to a plate.

Add the sliced garlic to the same oil and fry till light brown. Add the coriander roots and the cabbage. Fry till the cabbage is soft and translucent.

Add the glass vermicelli and stir fry. Add the sauces and chicken stock cube and simmer till the glass vermicelli is dry.

Add the bean sprouts and stir-fry briefly. Dish onto a plate and top with the fried prawns, fried shallots and coriander leaves.

While best eaten warm, it can also be enjoyed at room temperature with some Sambal Belacan and lime to accompany it.

ASSAM FISH CURRY

This is a sourish, spicy and appetizing dish which my Mum made regularly. This recipe is versatile and can be used for various types of fish like black pomfret, buttermilk fillets and stingray. There is a general view that expensive and fresh fish are to be steamed, whereas the rest should be deep fried or put in curry. This makes sense if you are running a food business but, for the home, cook your fish in whatever way you like.

As fish cooks quickly, it is important that you do not overcook it. The fish fillets should not be breaking apart.

400 g (14 oz) snapper fillets,
   skin removed
1 long brinjal (eggplant)
6 ladies fingers (okra)
1 sprig coriander leaves

Spice Paste
2 tbsps oil
10 shallots, sliced thinly
5 cloves garlic, sliced thinly
1 thumb-size turmeric, diced
   or 1 tsp turmeric powder
5 bird's eye chilli (*chilli padi*),
   diced or 2 tsps chilli paste
3 slices dried *Garcinia Cambogia*
   fruit (*assam keping*)
1 tsp salt
240 ml (1 cup) hot water
3 kaffir lime leaves
2 lemongrass bulbs

Slice the brinjal into bite-size chunks. Cut off the stems of the ladies fingers and slice the ladies fingers diagonally into two. Clean the fish.

Heat up the oil in a wok or pan. Put in the shallot and garlic slices, turmeric, chilli, *assam keping* and salt. Simmer for 5 minutes.

Crush the kaffir lime leaves with your fingers to release the fragrance and bruise the lemongrass bulbs. Add the hot water, the lemongrass and kaffir lime leaves to the spice paste.

When the curry is hot, add the the ladies fingers and brinjal. Simmer for 2 minutes then add the fish fillets. Cover the pot and simmer for another 2 minutes. Taste and adjust with more salt and tamarind sauce to your preference.

Turn off the heat and serve immediately or reheat if you are serving later. This is to prevent the fish from over cooking.

CURRIES

CURRIES ARE WELL-LOVED all around the world. Southeast Asian cuisines have evolved many popular curry-based recipes. If anything, every curry recipe is a mixture of influence of different cultures carried from port to port by trade and colonization. Merchants hawked their spices and herbs, and sailors and natives were inspired to evolve new recipes with ingredients from foreign lands.

From India, we have spices like cumin, coriander and cinnamon. From South America came chilli peppers. From Southeast Asia we have herbs like pandunus leaves, ginger, tamarind and lemongrass. Some early results of using herbs and spices from far and near are Nonya curries. To this day, this exotic and heady mixing of herbs, spices and chilies continue to inspire fusion recipes.

It has been said that there are as many curry recipes as there are households that cook them. We can understand why this is so as housewives use ingredients that she can find at home for her daily curries. Some of these creations eventually became popular in the community and were given names. The success of a curry in one food stall could result in it being duplicated elsewhere. A good example is Fish Head Curry which became known in Malaysia and Singapore in the 1950s. Being published in books, magazines and newspapers also popularized recipes and gave them an official name and place in our cuisine.

It is important to have a basic understanding of what makes a good curry.

Firstly, and this should be self-evident, use fresh spices and herbs. Their source is important, of course, as some countries or regions grow better spices than others. In the humid, tropical weather of Southeast Asia, extra care is also needed to keep spices and herbs fresh.

Assembling spice mixes yourself gives you more control and helps you to develop your palate and ability to recognize the difference which each spice makes to the recipe. All things being equal, spice seeds are generally fresher than store-bought ground spice. That said, if the ground mix is fresh, it can be very good too. So, while the recipes here call for you to assemble the spices yourself, if you are familiar with some good mixes, do use them. Sometimes, you simply have no local access to fresh spices, so you will just have to settle for powdered blends.

And whatever a cook may tell you, no single spice is mandatory for curry. If a recipe has a few types of spices and you are short of one, just leave it out.

Note that a bit of spice will go a long way in flavoring a curry. A common mistake which home cooks make is to imagine that adding water to curry powder will give you curry the way adding water to milk powder will give you milk. Most curries need a 'body' and this often comes from shallots or onions and other herbs like ginger or garlic. Onions will need to be slowly simmered in some oil to caramalise or sweat them to remove the sulfuric flavours and sweeten the paste. Sufficient oil is also needed for both mouth-feel and flavours, as most spices and chilies are oil-soluble rather than water-soluble.

Sufficient salt is also important. Salt enhances flavour and brings out the complexity of the curry. Leave out salt and your curry will be tasteless, no matter how much and how many types of spices you put into it. Add salt in stages, bearing in mind that the curry will thicken as water evaporates.

And whether you are using meat, potatoes or vegetables in your curries, the key is not to overcook them. Mushy meat has an unpleasant texture and overcooking means that a lot of flavours would have been released and lost from the meat.

The type of chilli you use will also affect the aroma of your curry. For this book, the chillies I refer to are the ones commonly found in markets and supermarkets.

Most curries are cooked in two stages. You first make the spice paste or *rempah* and then you add the meat.

To make the curry creamier, milk, coconut milk or yoghurt is used. If your curries already have good flavours from the spices, use the milk or coconut milk in moderation. Indian curries normally use yoghurt which adds a sour note and balances a good-flavoured curry very well. Evaporated milk is sometimes used too.

While a curry recipe tends to have a longer list of ingredients than recipes for other dishes, you don't need advanced culinary skills to make a good one. You can hardly ruin a curry. Even if you are new to cooking, give it a try. And if you think your first try wasn't great, remember that practice makes perfect.

IKAN SUMBAT
Chilli Fish

Chilli Fish, sometimes called Sambal Fish, is a dish with a WYSIWYG name. The mackerel is stuffed with sambal and deep fried. It is known in Malay as Ikan Sumbat (Stuffed Fish).

Whenever my Mum laid this dish on the table, we dropped whatever we were holding – literally. All inhibitions were cast away as we tore the fish apart the finger-lickin'-good way. It is the best way to eat this dish. Not only will it be more delicious, but your fingers are the best bone detectors.

Mum would eat and lick her fish cleaner than all of us. There is the flavourful, chilli-laced flesh to enjoy, the crunchy head and collar to suck and chew through, and the overflowing sambal chili to lap up. The leftover bones will look as if a cat had gone through the fish in a cartoon.

Traditionally, this Malay dish is made with *cencaru* or Hardtail Scad. The fish is not easily available in most wet markets. The skin is tough and the hard scales need to be removed (the fish monger can do this for you). It is great for this method of cooking or served in Assam Curry. The flesh is firm and the collar area is crispy when fried. This dish can also be made with other members of the Mackerel family like *kembong* (Indian Mackerel), *selar* (Scad) and, yes, even the larger *saba* mackerel which is popular with the Japanese.

I should add that my Mum preferred the sweetness of *selar* meat and this is the type of fish which she used often.

Properly fried, every part of the fish can be enjoyed. Serve it with sliced cucumber and rice.

This recipe is a good example of how a relatively cheap and ordinary fish can result in an appetizing meal in the hands of a good cook.

The sambal can also be cooked with ladies fingers or squid, so keep the extra for future use.

Ikan Sumbat

10 scad or makerel (*cencaru,*
   kembong or *selar*)

Spice Paste
6 lemongrass bulbs
30 shallots
5 cm (2 in) turmeric
15 chillies
5 bird's eye chillies (*chilli padi*)
1 tbsp shrimp paste (*belacan*)
1 tbsp sugar
2 tsps salt
3 kaffir lime leaves (*daun limau
   perut*), diced finely
2 tbsps oil for the sambal
Oil for deep-frying

Preparing the spice paste
Blend or pound coarsely the lemongrass, shallots,
turmeric and the two types of chilli into a paste. If your
paste is too fine, the texture will be wrong for this dish.
Toast the shrimp paste for a minute on a dry pan.

Heat up the wok and add the oil. After a minute, add the
blended paste and the toasted shrimp paste. Simmer for 5
minutes. Add the finely diced kaffir lime leaves. You don't
need to cook the sambal for a long time as you will be
deep-frying the stuffed fish.

Preparing the fish
Remove the gills of each fish. Gut the fish, removing all the
entrails from the gill cavity from the opening at the collar
without slitting the stomach, if you are able. You could get
your fishmonger to do this for you. The gall bladder, which
is bitter, is deeper in and you may have to stick your finger
in to remove that, but make sure not to break it. Clean the
stomach thoroughly.

Slit the back of the fish lengthwise on each side of the
dorsal fin. Cut midway into the fish – just before you hit
the spine – but not all the way to the stomach. Remember
that you are not filleting the fish but making two pockets
along the back of the fish.

Stuff the paste tightly into the two pockets and the
stomach from the collar opening. Leave the stuffed fishes
in the fridge for about an hour. The paste marinates the
fish and refrigeration dries the fish, making it easier to fry.

Frying the fish
Fry two or three fish at a time in a wok over medium fire.
Submerge only half of their bodies in oil. This will help to
keep most of the sambal in the fish better than if they are
completely submerged.

Tilt the wok gently from time to time to ensure that the
oil cooks the fish evenly. When the fish are three-quarter
cooked, turn them over. It will take about 15 minutes to
cook the fish. Bits of the stuffed chilli should be charred.

PAN-FRIED TURMERIC MACKEREL

Batang or Spanish Mackerel, marinated in turmeric powder was a comfort food in my childhood home. I recall it was also sold in Mum's restaurant and canteen. Over the years, *batang* has become more expensive but it is still a relatively cheap fish and is very suited for pan or deep frying as its flesh is firm.

A few tips about fish:
- As long as they are fresh, you won't need to do a lot to make them taste good.
- They keep well frozen and defrosts quickly.
- Fish do not need to be marinated for too long.
- Clean your fish thoroughly to remove the blood and scum.
- Fish bones and heads can be used to make stock.

If I am cooking this for a large dinner party, I will ask the fish monger to fillet it. This way you avoid having guests, who are busy chatting, choke on the bones. For family dinners, you can choose to have it as fish steaks or with bone in.

Pan-searing is preferred to cook small quantities of this fish as the direct contact with the pan will cause much of the marinade to stay on the fish. A thin layer of crust will also be formed.

As for the sauce, the sweet and savoury combination of *kecap manis* and fish sauce is a winner.

---

1 kg (2.2 lb) Spanish Mackerel
  (*batang*)
Cooking oil
Coriander leaves for garnishing

Marinade
1 tbsp turmeric powder
2 tsps salt
1 tsp white pepper
1 tbsp cornflour

Sauce
1 tbsp oil
1 coriander root and stems,
  smashed
2 stalks spring onions
3 dried chillies
200 ml (0.8 cup) Indonesian
  sweet sauce (*kecap manis*)
2 tbsps fish sauce
1 tbsp cornflour
240 ml (1 cup) water

Preparing the sauce
Heat 1 tbsp oil in a small pot. Add the smashed coriander root and stems, spring onions and dried chillies. Fry for 2 minutes. Include the sweet sauce and fish sauce. Prepare cornflour slurry by combining the cornflour with the water and add it slowly into the sauce, stirring vigorously as you do so. Taste to get the balance right. it should be sweet with a savory undertone. Strain the sauce.

Cooking the fish
Wash the fish thoroughly and slice it into steaks. Dry them with paper towels and marinate them for 30 minutes.

Heat up a pan over medium flame and add cooking oil to no more than 2 mm (0.7 in) in depth. When the oil is heated, put in the fish steaks. You should hear a sizzling sound. Cook each side for 2 minutes.

Serve the fish on the sauce or drenched with it. Garnish with some coriander leaves. This fried fish also goes very well with Sambal Belacan (page 229) or fresh chilli sauce (page 229).

DRY CHILLI CRAB IN BEAN PASTE

A cookbook to celebrate my Mum's legacy will not be complete without her favourite crab recipe. When my brother brought crabs from Ipoh, this is the dish she cooked.

The crabs caught in the rivers and swamps around Ipoh are generally smaller than other mud crabs – but the meat is sweet.

Cooked this way, the crabs pick up the sauce and ingredients like egg and curry leaves very well.

Seafood has to be cooked quickly over a strong fire. Given the limitations of a kitchen stove, deep fry the crabs first in smaller batches before doing the sauce and putting all the crabs back into the mix.

You can use this method for other crab dishes such as Black Pepper Crab.

2 kg (4.4 lb) crabs
250 ml (1 cup) oil
1 tbsp brown bean paste
2 tbsps chilli paste
2 tbsps dried shrimps
1 tbsp curry powder
10 slices ginger
5 cloves garlic, sliced
25 g (1 cup) curry leaves
1 cup water
1 tbsp sugar
1 tbsp soy sauce
2 eggs, lightly beaten
3 stalks spring onions, cut into
   2½-cm (1-in) lengths

Prepare and put in place all the ingredients, as the cooking time is brief.

Heat up the oil over medium to high heat and deep-fry the crabs in small batches till they are golden. Remove and set aside.

In 3 tablespoons of the oil that has been used for frying the crabs, fry the bean paste, chilli paste, dried shrimps, curry powder, ginger, garlic and curry leaves. After half a minute, pour in the water and simmer for 2 minutes. .

Put the crabs back in and mix them with the sauce. Add sugar and soy sauce. Stir fry for about 2 minutes. Add the eggs and spring onions. Stir fry for a minute and dish up.

Serve immediately.

SAMBAL SOTONG
Squid Sambal

Whenever my Mum made this, it was considered a special treat.

Squid is prized for its succulent texture. Flavorless on its own, it is often paired with flavourful sauces in Southeast Asian cuisine. I will almost always choose a squid dish at a Nasi Padang stall, especially Sambal Sotong or Sotong Goreng Hitam, squid cooked in its own black ink.

Cleaning squid is fast and simple. You can leave the skin on if you like, but skinning the squid is easy by using your nails to lift up the skin and then pulling it off with your fingers. Remember to remove the ink sac. Do give the squid a good wash with water or some lime or lemon juice to remove the slime.

The sambal for this dish is very similar to that for Nasi Lemak or Sambal Prawns. I will give you the recipe here but you can vary it. The essential ingredients are the chillies and onions. Variations will use combinations of blended lemongrass or kaffir lime leaves, toasted *belacan*, vinegar, tamarind paste or lime juice, sugar, and so on. Dried chillies have a deeper flavour and I prefer them over fresh chillies when I am preparing a sambal with seafood.

Squid can be easily overcooked. You may have heard of the 3- or 20-minute rule. You either cook it fast for under 3 minutes to get a succulent, crunchy texture or go beyond 20 minutes with a longer braise to tenderize it. If you cook it quickly at 55-57°C (131-135°F), it will be just right. At 60°C (140°F), it will shrink as the collagen layers contract.

1 kg (2.2 lb) large squids 6 large red onions 15 dried chillies, soaked 2 lemongrass bulbs 1 tsp shrimp paste (*belacan*) powder 200 ml (0.8 cup) oil 1 tsp salt 1 tsp sugar Lime juice to taste Cucumber, sliced Tomatoes, sliced Coriander leaves	Clean and wash the squids. Cut them into ½-cm (0.2-in) thick rings. Slice 3 of the onions into rings. Cut up the other 3 into chunks for the paste. Blend the soaked dried chilies, lemongrass bulbs along with the onion chunks into a fine paste. Heat up a wok. Toast the *belacan* first then add the oil. Follow with the paste and simmer for 15 minutes. Add the salt and sugar. Adjust to get the balance of taste you like. Add in the squid and onion rings. Stir. Remove after 2 minutes and plate. Splash on the lime juice and serve with fresh sliced cucumber and tomatoes, garnished with coriander leaves. You can cook the squid whole. Just place it in the sambal and simmer for 3 minutes, turning it occasionally. Cut it using scissors and serve it nicely plated with the slices arranged in the original shape of the squid.

VEGETABLES

MIXED VEGETABLES WITH CASHEW NUTS

This is one of the classic comfort foods that has stood the test of time. Mum called it Lup Lup, which is Cantonese for "small diced pieces". She often cooked the attractive, colourful dish for parties, accompanying the likes of Curry Chicken (page 39), Hakka Deep-Fried Pork (page 79) and rice. It is similar to the Italian Ratatouille. You can omit the chicken and prawns to go vegetarian. Once you have prepared the ingredients, the cooking is fast and easy. For this dish, texture is important. So don't overcook the dish. This mixed vegetable is also used as the filling for the fried yam basket dish.

As always, the quantities in this recipe are just a guide. Feel free to vary.

100 g (3.5 oz) prawn meat
300 g (10.5 oz) chicken meat
200 g (7 oz) fresh cashew nuts
8 baby sweet corn
1 green pepper (capsicum)
1 red pepper
2 medium red onions
2 tbsps cooking oil
3 cloves garlic, minced.
4 dried chillies
2 tsps cornflour made into a
　slurry with 2 tbsps water
Coriander leaves for garnishing

Marinade
1 tbsp oyster sauce
1 tsp light soy sauce
1 tsp fish sauce
1 tsp sugar
1 tbsp Chinese wine

Cut the prawn meat into small cubes.

Slice the chicken meat into 1-cm (0.4-in) cubes and marinate for 15 minutes. Meanwhile, slice the baby sweet corn into three pieces each. Also slice the peppers and red onions into bite-sized pieces. Rehydrate the chillies and slice them into 1 cm rings.

In a wok, heat 1 tablespoon of oil and fry the chillies till they are brown. Remove.

Add another tablespoon of oil and fry the cashew nuts until they turn golden brown. Note that some oil is necessary when cooking nuts in a wok or they will burn. Remove and set the nuts aside.

Using the leftover oil, fry the minced garlic. Then add the chicken along with all the marinade. Stir fry for 2 minutes, then add the vegetables and dried chillies. Stir fry for another 2 minutes before adding the wine and the cornflour slurry. Fry for a further 2 minutes.

Add the cashew nuts and garnish with the coriander leaves before serving.

This can be eaten at room temperature.

ACHIEVING *WOK HEI* IN THE HOME KITCHEN

WOK HEI, a Cantonese phrase that literally means "the wok's breath", describes the smoky taste obtained when food is cooked in a metal wok over very hot fire. The cook holds the wok in one hand and moves it about vigorously over the strong flames. Sometimes, this is done in combination with vigorous spatula action to move the food to the edge of the wok and tossing the food in the air by flicking the wok. The food will also catch some of the leaping flames directly, adding to the smokiness of the food. Mostly, it is about using high heat and a thin wok or one made of metal which is a good conductor to transfer heat to the food quickly.

It is, of course, not easy to cook this way at home, unless you have an outdoor kitchen with a high heat stove. However, you can still achieve it by using a good wok and cooking in smaller batches. I have made delicious Fried Rice and Hokkien Mee with *wok hei* without smoking up my kitchen. With skill and common sense, recipes that demand *wok hei* can be done well at home.

A two-phase cooking technique may be needed for some fried dishes. Seafood like crabs and prawns may need to be deep fried before being stir fried in a sauce. Seafood needs to be cooked quickly to prevent the meat from flailing – the cooked part of the meat breaking off from the uncooked part – or going mushy. By deep frying first, oil is used to increase the heat to the food to ensure quick and even cooking before it is flavoured with a sauce through stir frying.

Quite apart from the *wok hei*, a wok is a very good cooking tool. It is easy to cook big batches of vegetables or noodles with it as the large surface area allows for easy movement and good heat contact.

COLD TOFU IN BANGO SAUCE

Can a dinner dish be made in a minute?

The answer is yes when it comes to this side dish. My Mum had it regularly on our dinner table because of its convenience. You may be tempted to warm up the tofu but don't – the contrast between this cold dish and piping hot rice or soup is refreshing.

Kecap manis, widely used in Indonesian cuisine, is a syrupy, sweet, dark sauce made from black beans and palm sugar. Of all the brands, Bango is my favourite because it has a special aroma. Mixed with soy sauce, it is a delicious sweet-savory sauce for the tofu.

If you cannot find Bango, you can use other types of sweet sauces, including the sweetish Chinese dark soy sauce.

You should prepare this dish just before dinner starts. After all, it only takes a minute.

1 300-g (10.5-oz) block silken tofu
2 tbsps Bango *kecap manis*
2 tsps light soy sauce
2 tsps sesame oil or shallot oil
A dash of white pepper

Garnish
2 stalks spring onions, diced
1 tbsp fried shallots
1 chilli, diced

Mix the sauces and sesame or shallot oil in a bowl.

Open the packet of cold silken tofu, drain the water away and put the tofu on a plate.

Pour the sauce over it. Add a dash of white pepper, garnish with diced spring onions, fried shallots, and chilli.

Serve immediately.

CHAI CHOI
Braised Vegetables

This is a braised cabbage dish using *wong bok* (Napa cabbage) or the round green cabbage. The Nonya version includes *tau cheong* (salted soy beans) and Hokkiens will add fermented bean curd.

My mum used the milder-tasting white fermented bean curd or *fu yee* instead of *nam yee*, which is the red version though, as a general rule, the red one is for cooking and the white is for eating as an accompaniment. She also added shredded carrots for its sweetness and bean curd skin and vermicelli, both deep fried.

You can also add lily buds and dried sweet beancurd wafers (*tim chook*). During Chinese New Year, you can include "treasures" like dried oysters. When enriched, this dish is sometimes called Lohon Chai and is a regular feature at our reunion dinner table. Being a vegetarian dish, it was prepared for those who were abstaining from meat during the first two days of the new year.

I prefer the wok for cooking this dish as the heat is more even, I can stir easily and see what is going on. If you use a deep pot, it is likely that the heat will be higher at the bottom and the stuff there will be overcooked unless you stir more frequently. Look to see that the cabbage is soft enough, and use your taste buds as a guide.

Texture is another challenge as the cabbage can be too soft when overcooked. The pieces of cabbage should not break apart. Remember that even after you switch off the fire, the pot of food is still cooking.

It can be a very satisfying meal on its own, accompanied by rice and Sambal Belacan.

Chai Choi

1 large Chinese cabbage
(*wong bok*, Napa), cut into
broad strips
1 litre (4 cups) water or stock
100 g (3.5 oz) mung bean vermicelli (*fun see*),
deep fried
2 dried bean curd sticks (*fu chok*),
cut into 7½-cm (3-in) strips and
deep fried
8 Chinese dried mushrooms,
soaked and sliced
1 tbsp oyster sauce
2 thin slices of ginger
4 cubes (2 cm, 0.8 in) white
fermented beancurd, mashed
finely
1 tsp salt, or to taste
3 tbps vegetable oil
2 carrots, shredded
15 small black fungus, soaked
and cut into pieces
Coriander leaves

Lightly deep fry separately the mung bean vermicelli and beancurd sticks and set aside.

Braise mushrooms and dried oysters together in some water with the oyster sauce and soy sauce over a low fire for about 30 minutes.

Heat the oil in a wok and fry the ginger till golden brown.

Add the white fermented beancurd and stir fry briskly until aromatic.

Put in the black fungus, carrot, cabbage and stir fry briskly for 2 minutes. Add the stock or water, bring to a boil, and simmer for 10 minutes.

Add the braised mushrooms, beancurd sticks and simmer for 10 more minutes. Taste and adjust with salt, adding some light soy sauce if you wish.

Finally, add the deep fried bean vermicelli. Stir a bit more and switch off the fire.

Serve hot in a bowl, garnished with coriander leaves and accompanied by a small plate of Sambal Belacan and a bowl of steaming rice.

SOME OF THE DRIED INGREDIENTS WHICH CAN BE USED FOR CHAI CHOI OR LOHON CHAI.
FROM LEFT: DRIED OYSTERS, BEANCURD STICKS, MUNGBEAN OR GLASS VERMICELLI, DRIED FUNGUS, BLACK MOSS AND DRIED MUSHROOMS.

CHOI KEOK
Chinese Mustard Green Stew

If there is a festive dish which captures the Chinese New Year season for the Wong family, it has to be this hot and sour Hakka soup. My Mum made it in a large pot on the second day of the New Year. The base of the stock is meaty and to that, tamarind sauce, dried chillies, and mustard greens are added. The recipe is a variation of the Nonya classic soup, Itik Tim or Kiam Chye Ark (Duck and Salted Mustard Greens Soup).

Leftover meats and bones – plentiful by the second day of feasting – are used. Roast duck bones and roast pork is great for the stock. To that, you add some fresh pork bones and chicken feet. The Cantonese name of this dish, Choi Keok (literally, vegetables and feet to mean leftovers) describes this dish well.

There are two types of mustard greens, the round-stem version, and the leafy variety. As the latter's leafy texture makes for good eating, it is more popular. Mustard greens are almost tasteless on their own. However, it absorbs flavours very well, sponging up anything you cook with it, resulting in a luscious texture. So, it is the perfect vegetable for this dish.

If you can't find fresh mustard greens, you can use *hum choy*, either the round-stemmed or leafy, brined version. Soak it in water for half and hour or more. You may need to soak it in 2 or more batches of fresh water to remove the saltiness.

Dried chillies are important to this dish to make it slightly spicy. For the sourness, add *assam keping*. A good meat stock needs at least 2 hours of simmering. If you have a pressure cooker, you can cut down the time by a third.

Don't let Chinese New Year end without cooking this at least once. After all, you need to do something with your leftovers. The wonderful thing about Choi Keok is that the 'second rate' meat becomes very good.

As I reflect on this, I think of the verse from the Bible in Ecclesiastes 3:10a which says "He has made everything beautiful in its time."

Yes, God specializes in turning nothing into something. This leftover stew reminds me of this. If you think your life's usefulness has been exhausted, think again. In His hands, the best is yet to be.

As we are using leftovers, it is not helpful to quantify the ingredients but I will give you quantities just as a guide.

Choi Keok

5 litres (1.3 gal) water
1 roast duck or leftover meats
10 dried chillies
4 slices dried *Garcinia Cambogia* fruit (*assam keping*)
200 g (7 oz) tamarind pulp (*assam*), rendered in 240 ml (1 cup) water, seeds removed
4 stalks round-stemmed mustard greens
2 stalks leafy mustard greens
Salt and rock sugar to taste

In a pot of boiling water, blanch the meat and bones for 10 minutes. It is important to do this to reduce the fat. Do not use roast duck heads or necks as they have strong flavours and your soup will taste awful by the second day.

Heat up the water in a pot. Add the blanched meat and bones. Simmer for 30 minutes.

Add the chopped mustard greens and simmer for another hour or so. The texture of the vegetables needs to be soft and yet have a nice bite to it. Towards the end, adjust the taste to your liking with the rock sugar, tamarind liquid and salt.

This is best eaten the day after it is cooked as the flavors will continue to develop. We will normally leave it overnight on the stove. Just boil it and leave it undisturbed. This pot can be 'rolled over' for a few days, with more meat or veg added. While you can add other vegetables into the pot, I advise that you stick to just mustard greens. I will not add any leftover Chinese sausages or fish bones. These will spoil the taste. Yes, use your leftovers but not any leftover.

PENANG ROJAK
Penang Style Fruit and Vegetable Salad

Rojak is a Malay word for "mixture." It is also the name of a salad of fruits and vegetables coated in a sweet and savoury sauce.

There are many different types of Rojak. The recipe below is more common in Malaysia and Singapore, where a dark and sticky sweet sauce is used. It is sometimes called Penang Rojak. The sauce is a combination of Tim Cheong (brown soya bean-based sweet sauce, page 234), the black and sticky shrimp sauce (*har kou* or *petis udang*), sugar, chilli paste and *belacan* (shrimp paste). Crushed peanuts and sesame seeds are also added. The key to a good Rojak is the sauce. I will recommend that you make you own Tim Cheong as it is much better than commercial ones.

The sauce for the Rojak should be mixed when needed. It is best to prepare the various ingredients and put it together *a la minute*. The recipe below takes this approach.

This type of Rojak can be served as an appetiser or a dessert.

1 yambean (jimcama, *bangkwang*)
1 small ripe pineapple
1 guava
1 unripe mango (optional)
1 cucumber
1 green apple (optional)
2 jambu (optional)
1 torch ginger bud (*bunga kantan*)
Prawn Fritters (see page 213, optional)
200 g (7 oz) water convulvulous (*kangkung*), blanched (optional)
Bean sprouts (optional)

For the sauce
Tim cheong (see page 234)
Shrimp sauce (*har kou*, *petis udang*)
Shrimp paste (*belacan*), ground
Sugar
Chilli paste
Peanuts, toasted and crushed
Sesame seeds, toasted

Peel the yambean, pineapple, guava and mango, if using, and cut into rough bite-sized pieces.

Cut the cucumber, apple and jambu into bite-sized pieces. Leave the skin on for colour.

Dice the torch ginger bud finely.

Toast the shrimp paste and pound into granules.

In a deep salad bowl, put in equal amounts of the vegetables, fruit and prawn fritters if using, about 40 pieces in all. For this portion, add half a teaspoon of ground belacan, 2 tablespoons of *tim cheong*, 1 tsp of prawn paste, 1 tsp of sugar, 1 tsp of chilli paste, 2 tablespoons of crushed toasted peanuts and 1 teaspoon of sesame seeds. Toss, and adjust, if necessary, to get the balance to your preference. The sauce should be sweet with a savoury undertone. The level of spiciness from the chilli is up to you. The sauce should coat each piece of the ingredients.

Garnish with more crushed peanuts and diced torch ginger bud, and serve immediately.

FRIED BRINJAL IN BELADO SAUCE

Brinjal. Eggplant. Aubergine. Depending on where you live, it bears a different name. It also comes in many different shapes: round, oval and long. One thing is certain, it is popular in many cuisines and there are many ways to cook it.

What makes brinjals delicious is the crisped skin and creamy, luscious flesh. Retaining the beautiful violet hue can be challenging as they lose their colour when they are heated and oxidize. To prevent them from becoming mushy and lose their colour when cooked, deep fry or cook them in hot oil first. You can then coat them in any sauce you wish after deep frying.

This recipe uses the Belado, a popular Indonesian sambal (see page 231). As you can imagine, many other sauces go well with deep fried brinjals.

This dish cooks quickly and is best assembled *a la minute*.

3 medium-sized brinjals
4-5 tbsps Sambal Belado
  (see page 231)
240 ml (1 cup) cooking oil
1 stalk spring onions, chopped
Fried shallots

Cut the brinjal into 6 cm (2½ in) pieces.

Heat up the Sambal Belado sauce in a small pot.

Heat the oil in a wok or pan. When it is hot, add the brinjal chunks and stir fry, constantly coating it with oil. Remove the brinjal and plate it.

Add the warmed Sambal Belado sauce and garnish with the chopped spring onions and fried shallots. Serve immediately.

HAKKA YONG TAU FOO
Hakka Stuffed Vegetables

It was Levi Strauss who said: "The process of cooking is the process by which nature is turned into culture."

Nothing can be more true when it comes to Hakka Yong Tau Foo. In the hands of a Hakka cook, some common and ordinary ingredients were mixed, chopped, stuffed, steamed, boiled and fried to create a classic culinary masterpiece.

So, when it's Yong Tau Foo, it is Hakka, much like how Chicken Rice is Hainanese.

This was amongst the first few dishes I made when I tried to recreate the taste of home in the early years after my move to Singapore. Not only is it delicious, it is a great party dish, especially when served with Chee Cheong Fun. It is not an expensive dish and your guests will be impressed by it.

Stuffing
For about 100 Hakka Yong Tau Foo items

Hakka Yong Tau Foo stuffing is made from pork, fish, salted fish, garlic, spring onions, cornflour, salt and water. Use pork with some fat to ensure that the filling is moist and tasty. Do not use the skin. Ask the butcher to grind the meat once.

The bouncy texture comes from the fish, not the pork. Therefore, choosing the right fish is important. Spanish mackerel (*batang*) is good for Hakka Yong Tau Foo, though Wolf Herring (*parang* or *sai tow*) works too. I prefer *batang* as it is very easy to scrape the meat off with a large spoon. The bones go into the soup stock. Another alternative is Yellowtail Scad (*selar*).

As for salted fish, the softer *mui heong* variety is preferred. Use the superior type that is normally stored cold when sold.

250 g (0.9 oz) minced pork
500 g (1.1 lb) fish paste
½ tsp salt
50 g (1.75 oz) salted fish
1 tbsp minced garlic
2 tbsps diced spring onions
2 tbsps cornflour
1 tsp white pepper
100 ml (0.4 cup) water

You mix everything together and mince it with a chopper (or two!). Apart from mixing the ingredients, this will also add some 'bounce' to the texture. Chop the stuffing mixture for at least 20 minutes.

Shape some of the mixture into a meatball and deep fry it. Take a bite to taste. Is the texture and flavour to your liking? Adjust if you need to. If it is too salty, you have to add more meat or fish to the stuffing. If the texture is too soft, chop it for a few more minutes. Once you get it right, you will hardly need to test it again as long as you make notes to this recipe and follow them.

With the stuffing ready, the rest of your Hakka Yong Tau Foo is simply waiting to happen.

Stuffed Bitter Gourd

Slice the bitter gourd at a slant so that the pieces will hold the stuffing better. It can be difficult for the stuffing to cling to the bitter gourd when it is being cooked as the bitter gourd will soften. To minimize this problem, remove the inner lining when you remove the seeds as this lining will give way easily when cooked and loosen the stuffing.

There are a few ways to cook stuffed bitter gourd.

Braising in sauce
This is a good way to cook stuffed bitter gourd, especially when you are serving Hakka Yong Tau Foo with rice. Heat up a wok or pot, and add a tablespoon of oil. Add some diced garlic, black bean sauce, sugar and some water. Taste to adjust. Add the stuffed bitter gourd and gently braise for 20 minutes. This is a favourite Hakka way of cooking this, although I won't normally do it for an already elaborate Hakka Yong Tau Foo line-up.

Cooking in soup
After you have made the soup (page 151), add the stuffed bitter gourd to simmer for 20 minutes. Note that the soup will have a bittery taste. It is fantastic when eaten with rice.

Deep-frying
Sometimes, I will deep fry the stuffed bitter gourd. Do it for about 15 minutes. Serve with some savory sauce (page 151), garnished with some diced spring onions.

Stuffed Fresh Chillies

Stuffed chillies are delicious if you cook them right. Like roasted green peppers, caramelized fresh chillies take on a sweetness when cooked on high heat. Chillies will cook faster than roasted pepper as they are thinner.

Use both red and green chillies. Choose the larger and fatter ones for easier stuffing. Slit along the chilli, leaving 1½ cm (0.6 in) on both ends uncut. De-seed using the handle end of a spoon, then fill the pocket created with stuffing.

Shallow pan fry over medium heat with a very thin layer of oil. You may need to press the chilli down and hold it in place with a pair of long chopsticks so that it is in direct contact with the hot surface of the pan. It will take about 2 minutes to cook.

When properly cooked, the texture of the stuffed chilli should be soft, not crunchy, and yet firm enough to be picked up whole by a pair of chopsticks. The chillies should have some charred spots.

You can serve them on a thin layer of brown sauce (page 151, garnished with diced spring onions.

Fried Stuffed Brinjals

Stuffed brinjal is fantastic. Its slightly bitter taste and creamy texture combines wonderfully with the savory stuffing. The shape of the diagonally sliced brinjal is a ready receptor for the stuffing. When the sides are charred and caramelized, the texture and aroma of the brinjal changes.

Stuffing the brinjal pieces
Use the long type of brinjal. Cut it into 3-cm pieces at an angle to create a thick oval piece. It needs to be thick enough so that you can enjoy the contrast of the crisped skin, the soft flesh, and the meaty filling.

Cut a slit in each slice of brinjal to create a pocket. Prepare a bowl of the stuffing and another with some flour and water. Spoon in stuffing into the pocket. As the stuffing is sticky, wet the spoon in the bowl of water and flour and use it to smoothen the filling. Leave it to dry in the open before you fry it.

Frying the brinjal pieces
I prefer the patient technique of shallow pan frying rather then deep frying. This way, the direct contact with the pan will sear and crisp the flesh of the brinjal and stuffing while retaining some of the beautiful purple of the skin. Coat the pan with a very thin layer of oil – no more than 1 mm. When it is hot enough, fry small batches of stuffed brinjal. It should take no more than 5 minutes to cook a batch.

If you are making a huge batch for 120 people, as I have done a few times, you will have to use deep frying. Just make sure that the oil is so hot that it is shimmering and fry quickly. Don't overcrowd. About 3 minutes per batch will do.

It is best to serve this stuffed brinjal hot off the pan. If you need to fry them ahead of service, just warm them up by searing batches quickly on a dry pan or a quick deep fry before serving.

You pick up a piece of brinjal with a pair of chopsticks. Your teeth meets the crispy skin before hitting the moist, soft flesh and finally the savory center, completing the first bite. Amazing. I think brinjal was created for Hakka Yong Tau Foo.

Beancurd Rolls

Beancurd roll is another favourite item of Hakka Yong Tau Foo.

Which type of dried beancurd skin should you get? I like to use *foo chook*, the beancurd sheets which are normally used for desserts. The reason is simple: these come in large, flat sheets of regular size so that is easier to divide them into rectangular portions. I will not use the very salty variety that is normally used for Ngoh Hiang (spiced meat rolls). It is not worth the effort to remove the salt nor does it taste good for Hakka Yong Tau Foo.

To prepare the *foo chook*, you need to first wet them so that they become soft and able to be shaped and folded. Dip each sheet into a tray of water or wipe it with a wet cloth. When pliable, snip into rectangle portions of about 6 x 10 cm (2.4 x 4 in), the long side with the grain. The actual size depends on the size and shape of the bean curd sheet you have because you want to use it all up. Waste not, want not.

Spread a portion of the stuffing on a cut piece of *foo chook*. Roll along the grain to make a flattened cigar. The stuffing will hold the beancurd together, so spreading some near the edges will make it easier to form the parcels.

Some prefer a layered roll. Others, a thick stuffing in the center. It's up to you. Rest the roll with its weight on the edge of the wrapping to hold it down. Pat dry the stuffed beancurd rolls or leave it in the open to dry up a bit as that will make the frying and crisping easier.

Heat up some oil in a wok. You know it is hot enough when a bit of beancurd skin thrown into it sizzles. The skin will crisp and firm up when it is deep fried, so each parcel should only be cooked for about a minute or less. Shake off excess oil as you lift the rolls up with a sieve or chopsticks.

Stuffed Deep-fried Beancurd Puffs

Deep-fried beancurd puffs or *tau foo pok* crisps up nicely when fried. They normally come in cubes.

Make a slit, add the stuffing and deep fry. You can also make "Inverted *tau foo pok*". Fold the *tau foo pok* inside out and add the stuffing. Both versions are very easy to prepare.

Stuffed Ladies Fingers

Ladies fingers add some greens to your Hakka Yong Tau Foo line-up.

Slit each lengthwise to create a pocket. You do not need to remove the seeds. Push the lines of seeds to one side as you put in the stuffing. Deep fry the ladies fingers briefly and then simmer them in the soup or fish stock for about 20 minutes.

Soup for Hakka Yong Tau Foo

I will always make a fish soup from the head and bones of the fish used to make the stuffing. You need the well-flavoured stock to cook certain Hakka Yong Tau Foo items: *Tau foo pok*, bittergourd and brinjal. Of course you can serve the soup with Hakka Yong Tau Foo and rice.

2 fish heads and bones
300 gm (10.5 oz) yellow soy beans
Light soy sauce to taste

Clean the fish head and bones with water, washing off any trace of blood and innards. Simmer it along with the soy beans in 4 litres (1 gal) of water for about 30 minutes over low flame. Cook the Hakka Yong Tau Foo items in it (i.e. bittergourd, brinjal or *tau foo pok*). Note that you are flavoring the soup with them as you do so. If the soup is not savory enough, add some light soy sauce.

Sauces for Hakka Yong Tau Foo

Sauces should not be an afterthought for Hakka Yong Tau Foo. You might offer the savoury sauce below and Chilli Sauce (page 228).

SAVOURY SAUCE

2 tbsps oil
2 tbsps cornflour
1 tbsp oyster sauce
1 tsp sugar
240 ml (1 cup) water

Heat up the oil in a wok and add the cornflour and stir to create a *roux.* Then add the oyster sauce, sugar and water. Stir till you get a smooth, translucent paste.

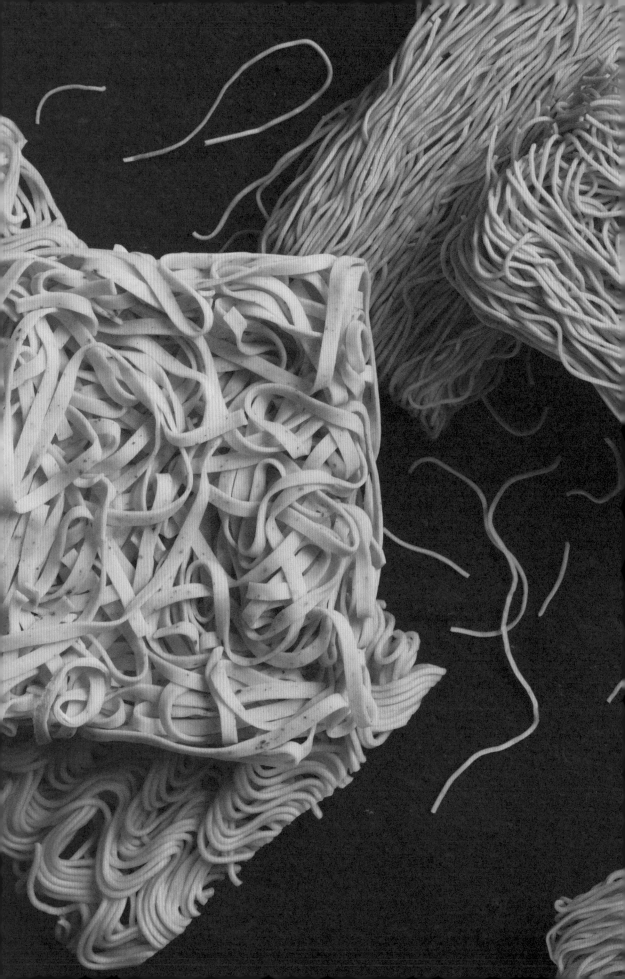

NOODLES

FRIED RICE VERMICELLI

Rice vermicelli, *mai fun* in Cantonese or *bee hoon* in Hokkien is a 'stand by me' friend which every Chinese home cook should get familiar with. I ate a lot of it growing up, second only to rice. Being made from rice explains its appeal as a staple to Asians. It should not be confused with cellophane noodles known as *toong fun* (Cantonese) or *tang hoon* (Hokkien) that are made from mung beans.

Like pasta for Italians, Asians cook *mai fun* in many ways and for different occasions, grand and homely. Dehydrated like pasta, it can keep for months in your larder. You need to soak it in water for 20-30 minutes, depending on the thickness, to rehydrate them. After that, you can choose to fry it, mix it in some sauces or add it to soup.

Unlike pasta, it absorbs liquid and flavours well. This opens up many ways of cooking *mai fun*, and indeed there are countless good and established recipes using the noodle.

Fried Rice Vermicelli is very popular for parties as it tastes good even when served at room temperature. It also accompanies many dishes very well. It can be served with Chicken Curry (page 40), Fried Chicken Wings (page 33) and Chai Choi (page 131). It can also be a stand alone vegetarian dish with strips of carrots, slices of cabbage and French green beans added.

Mai fun can also be enjoyed in soups. The name Penang Hae Mee (page 173) is in a way misleading because rice vermicelli is an essential ingredient for it. It picks up the flavours of the soup very well. In Singapore, Crab Bee Hoon and White Bee Hoon are very popular, as is Mee Siam which also uses rice vermicelli.

Here, I will share with you a very basic and simple recipe to get you acquainted with *mai fun*. Once you have built up your confidence, you can try some more elaborate recipes and create your own too.

Fried Rice Vermicelli

SERVES 5

200 g (7 oz) dried rice vermicelli
   (*mai fun*, *bee hoon*)
2 tbsps oil or lard
1 tbsp chopped garlic
1 egg
1 tbsp dark soy sauce
1 tbsp soy sauce
1 tbsp fish sauce
200 ml (⁴/₅ cup) water
200 g (7 oz) bean sprouts
White pepper
Sambal or chilli sauce

Garnish
Coriander leaves
Fried shallots

Soak the *mai fun* in a pot of water for 20 minutes. Remove it and put it in a strainer for the water to drip away. Soaking it makes it easier to handle the *mai fun*. Some thicker varieties of *mai fun* will need longer soaking. If you use warm water, the soaking time will be shorter.

Heat up a wok and add the oil. Add the garlic and the egg, and fry for about half a minute.

Put in the rehydrated *mai fun*, using your hands to separate the strands as you do so such that the noodles are not entangled.

Add the sauces, and water and stir.

After 5 minutes, move the *mai fun* to the side of the wok and add the bean sprouts. Do a quick fry and mix together. It should be done in about 10 minutes,

Test the texture of the *mai fun*. You can often tell how cooked it is just by lifting some of the noodles using chopsticks and observing how they drape. Make sure it is not too soft.

Garnish with coriander leaves, fried shallots and sprinkle on some white pepper. Serve with some sambal or chilli sauce on the side. Fried *mai fun* can be served warm or at room temperature.

THAI FRIED RICE VERMICELLI

This is an appetizing, sourish fried *bee hoon* or *mai fun* recipe which my Mum cooked very often, especially for parties. It makes good use of unique indigenous herbs like *bunga kantan*, the torch ginger bud. She called it "Thai style" as Tom Yam paste is used. I see it as a Northern Malaysian take on Fried Rice Vermicelli.

SERVES 5

200 g (7 oz) dried rice vermicelli (*mai fun*, *bee hoon*)
500 g (1.1 lbs) bean sprouts
500 g (1.1 lbs) cabbage, diced
6 black fungus, soaked and shredded
300 g (10.5 oz) chicken meat, sliced
400 g (14 oz) small prawns, de-shelled
1 bunch Chinese celery, chopped
2 torch ginger buds (*bunga kantan*), diced finely
240 ml (1 cup) water

Sauce
2 tsps Tom Yam sauce
3 tsps chilli sauce
1 tbsp brown soy bean paste
2 tsps dark soy sauce

Rehydrate the *mai fun* for 30 minutes in water.

Heat up 1 tsp of oil in a wok and fry the bean sprouts for about a minute and set aside.

Heat up 1 tbsp of oil in the same wok, put in the sauces, and stir fry.

Add the diced cabbage and shredded black fungus and fry for about a minute.

Include the chicken and prawns and fry for about 2 minutes before adding the bean sprouts, Chinese celery and the diced torch ginger buds. Then, add the *mai fun* and fry till it is dry. The *mai fun* will pick up some water it has been soaking in as you transfer it to the wok. So, add more water only if you think it is necessary. It is harder to fry *mai fun* if it is too dry.

This dish can be served at room temperature.

THE GOODNESS OF NOODLES

NOODLES ARE THE ULTIMATE comfort food for many Asians. When we travel, we will eventually end up craving for it, whether in thick sauces, spicy or light stocks, or umami-laden seafood broths.

There are generally two types of noodles: wheat-based and rice-based. The popular yellow noodles (*meen*) are wheat-based. The rice ones, like vermicelli (*mai fun* or *mee hoon*) and flat noodles (*hor fun*) are lighter. The type of the noodles determine which recipes they go with.

One of my favourite breakfast noodles is the 'economy noodles' or, as my Mum called it in Cantonese, *keng chai mai fun*. It is a combination of wheat noodle and rice vermicelli fried in some soy sauce accompanied with a chilli sauce.

I grew up eating noodles made by my Mum such as Prawn Noodles (page 173), Mee Rebus (page 165), and Assam Laksa (page 179). These recipes are more elaborate and they are great for parties. On those days when she cooked them, there was always an air of excitement as family and friends gathered. The extra effort put into making a good broth is worth the while when guests – slurping and burping – look satisfied and comforted.

Mum's noodle recipes bring back many lovely memories of the gathering of friends and family.

Don't let the long list of ingredients in the noodle recipes put you off. If you are starting out, the Ipoh Kai See Hor Fun's broth (page 160) is the easiest to make. Often, simple can be very good and a few ingredients are all you need.

The various recipes for dry noodles are fast and easy to make. Like dressings for salads, the flavours comes from an emulsion of sauces and oils. Use good sauces – premium soy sauce or oyster sauce – and good flavoured oils like onion oil, sesame oil, lard or chilli oil. In dry noodles, as there is no soup or stock, the flavours are more intense. Garnish with fried shallots or use a good chilli paste. You do not need many ingredients to flavour dry noodles. Just find a good balance.

Once you learn to make the sauces or stocks and organise yourself well, in no time, you will find the confidence to entertain guests. When you are ready for the summit, serve Assam Laksa.

IPOH KAI SEE HOR FUN
Ipoh Style Flat Rice Noodles in Chicken Broth

This is a lovely Cantonese flat rice noodle dish which originated from Ipoh in Malaysia. The broth is a chicken-based stock with some prawns added for flavour. The tasty, light broth accompanies the silky smooth Ipoh *hor fun* very well. Strips of chicken meat, slices of prawn, chives, bean sprouts and fried shallots add texture and flavour to it.

This is one of the simpler noodle dishes which my Mum made regularly. Unlike the heavy, fat-based *ramen* or Penang Prawn Mee, this dish goes the opposite direction with a clean, light broth to match the delicate *hor fun*.

There is some prawn/chicken oil in it, but it should not be so much that it becomes cloying. Chicken meat will impart more flavour to the stock then just bones alone. I use a large, whole chicken to make the broth. One thing which you should never do is to use commercial chicken stock as a base for this soup. This recipe does not use any pork or lard at all.

If you can get genuine Ipoh *hor fun*, you should definitely use it. If not, get the best flat rice noodles available.

Serves 10-12

2 kg (4.4 lb) flat rice noodles
  (*hor fun*)
1 kg (2.2 lb) medium-sized
  prawns
4 litres (1 gal) water
1 large chicken, preferably,
  kampong or free-range chicken
2 tbsps sugar or equivalent
  amount of rock sugar
Salt to taste
2 tbsps sesame oil
10 stalks chives
500 g (17.5 oz) bean sprouts

Fried shallots for garnishing
Cut red chillies in light soy sauce

Making the broth
Peel the prawns, de-vein and set aside. Reserve the prawn heads and shells.

Bring the water to a boil and add the chicken, sugar and salt. Allow to simmer.

Meanwhile, in a wok or pot, fry the prawn heads and shells in 2 tablespoons of sesame oil till they turn golden. Then add to the pot of stock. Later, this will impart a layer of red oil to the stock.

When the chicken is cooked, remove some of the chicken breast and thigh meat and set aside. Continue to simmer the stock for an hour to extract more flavour from the chicken.

Taste and adjust with more sugar or salt as you prefer. Strain to finish the broth.

Preparing the topping
Using your fingers, tear the reserved chicken meat into strips. Avoid slicing.

Blanch the prawn meat in the soup. Remove, and after it has cooled, slice the prawns into two, lengthwise.

Cut the chives into 2½-cm (1-in) lengths. Blanch for half a minute.

Assemby
Blanch a portion of *hor fun* and bean sprouts in a pot of boiling water for about 10 seconds and put them in a bowl. Pour the boiling broth over.

Place a few pieces of the cooked prawns, chicken and chives on top of the noodles.

Garnish with fried shallots and serve immediately. Don't forget the small plate of light soy sauce with cut red chillies.

MEE REBUS
Noodles in Potato Broth

Mee Rebus is a Malay dish, where yellow wheat noodles are eaten in a thick, potato-based broth along with condiments.

My Mum's verison has its origin from the small town of Teluk Intan in West Malaysia, where it is served with Prawn Fritters (page 213) and Cuttlefish Sambal (page 167). She learned this dish from her close friend and companion chef.

I have never tasted a plate of Mee Rebus as good as Mum's. The flavours, the balance, and the different textures come together magically. Her recipe here is spot on. When I first made it, eating it was going down memory lane. We have Mum to thank for that.

Mum's recipe uses dried anchovies (*ikan bilis*) rather than dried shrimps (*ha mai* or *hae bee*), resulting in a broth which does not have the sharper taste of dried shrimps. Crunchy fresh green chilies, bean sprouts and Chinese parsley finish the dish very well.

The Prawn Fritters are best eaten with the broth though you will have difficulty restraining hungry guests from going at it first as a snack.

Mee Rebus

Serves 20

3 kg (6.6 lb) thick yellow noodles
1½ kg (3.3 lb) bean sprouts
2 kg (4.4 lb) yellow potato

Ikan bilis broth
500 g (1.1 lbs) dried anchovies
    (*ikan bilis*), heads off and bodies
    rinsed
6 litres (1.5 gal) water

Spice paste
30 dried chillies, soaked in hot
    water (alternatively use chilli
    paste)
5 candlenuts (*buah keras*)
20 shallots
6 lemongrass bulbs
1 tsp chopped turmeric
240 ml (1 cup) cooking oil
500 g (17.5 oz) tomato sauce
200 g (7 oz) peanuts, skinned

Flavouring for soup
4 tbsps sugar
2 chicken stock cubes
1 tbsp salt
400 g (14 oz) tamarind pulp
    (*assam*) mixed with enough
    water to form a liquid paste
2 tbsps cornflour

Preparing the *ikan bilis* broth
Fill the stock pot with the water. Add the *ikan bilis* and simmer for 45 minutes. Strain the broth.

Preparing the spice paste
Grind or blend the spices and herbs finely to make the *rempah* (spice paste).

Heat up the oil in a wok. Add the *rempah* and tomato sauce and simmer for about 20 minutes. Reserve 2 tablespoons of the *rempah* for the cuttlefish and add the rest to the pot of anchovy broth.

Grind the peanuts finely and add it to the broth.

Preparing the potatoes
Peel the potatoes and cut them into small cubes.

Add them to the broth and simmer till the potato cubes are soft.

Use a stick blender to puree the potatoes in the broth. Alternatively, cook the potatoes in some water till soft and use a blender to puree it before adding it to the broth.

Flavouring the soup
This final phase of finishing off the flavours of the soup requires you to taste and adjust according to what you like. Use the amounts of flavouring given as a rough guide. The soup should be sweet with a salty and sour undertone. Adding cornflour will thicken the soup but bear in mind that as you simmer the soup, it will thicken.

Cuttlefish sambal
2 cuttlefish
20 shallots or red onions, sliced
240 ml (1 cup) chilli paste
2 tbsps oil
3 tsps sugar
1 tsp salt
2 tbsps spice paste
1 cup crushed roasted peanuts

Prawn Fritters
See page 213

Garnishes
2 pieces extra-firm tofu (*tau korn*)
12 eggs, hard-boiled
1 bunch Chinese parsley
10 green chilies
10 limes, halved.

Preparing the sambal cuttlefish
Slice the cuttlefish into bite-size pieces. Heat up some water in a wok or pot and, when boiling, blanch the cuttlefish for 20-30 seconds.

Heat up the oil a wok and fry the sliced shallots, the reserved *rempah*, and chilli paste for 15 minutes. Add the crushed roasted peanuts, sugar, and salt.

Turn off the fire and add the cuttlefish. Stir to mix. If you overcook the cuttlefish, they will harden.

Preparing the Prawn Fritters
See page 213.

Preparing the garnishes
Slice the extra-firm tofu into thin slices.

Cut the green chillies into rounds for the crunch and heat.

Chop up some Chinese parley. Don't confuse this with coriander leaves, which are shorter. Chinese parsley go really well with this dish.

Peel and halve the hard-boiled eggs

Serving the Mee Rebus
Prepare the Mee Rebus plate by plate.

Blanch one portion of noodles and a generous amount of bean sprouts in a pot of boiling water.

Plate the noodles and bean sprouts and pour on the hot broth to cover half of the noodles.

Top it with the Prawn Fritters, Cuttlefish Sambal, eggs, sliced green chillies, Chinese parsley, and *tau korn*. Serve immediately.

PAN MEE
Pinched Noodles

This flat noodle served in a clear broth is popular today and considered a healthy option. I grew up eating my Mum's version, where the flat noodles are flattened and pinched by hand. So they will be in rough pieces with uneven thickness. This is the character of the dish, as opposed to uniform machine-made noodles. The unevenness adds a varying *al dente* texture which makes these noodles unique and enjoyable.

It is easy to do this at home as the broth is quick and simple to prepare, and mixing and kneading the dough is not as messy as it sounds. One good thing about making your own noodles is that you can make as much as you need and nothing needs to be wasted.

Sufficient kneading is important to get the chewy or *al dente* texture. Kneading this flour-water mixture is not much different from doing the dough for bread and pasta.

If you prefer your noodles to be very thin and flat, you can put pieces in cold water and flatten them before boiling.

Fried anchovies are essential to this recipe. While you can add fried lardon, pieces of minced pork will go better. As for vegetables, the very ordinary *choi sum* (mustard green) or *wong bok* (Napa cabbage) goes very well with it.

Pan Mee

Serves 6

Broth
1 kg (2.2 lb) pork ribs
1 small chicken, skinned
170 g (1 cup) soy beans (optional)
1 chicken stock cube
1 tsp salt
5 litres water

For making noodles
500 g (1.1 lbs) plain flour
150 ml (³/₅ cup) water
1 tsp salt
1 tbsp oil

Toppings
300 g (10.5 oz) dried anchovies
  (*ikan bilis*)
100 g (3.5 oz) dried shitake
  mushrooms
300 g (10.5 oz) minced pork
2 cloves garlic, diced
6 tsps fried shallots
Oil for deep frying
1 tsp oyster sauce
½ tsp dark soy sauce
White pepper to taste

Making the broth
Heat up the water for the broth in a deep pot. Add the other broth ingredients and simmer for 1 hour.

Making the noodles
Add oil and salt to the flour. Slowly add water and knead. You need to knead it into a smooth dough and you will know it is done when the dough no longer sticks to your hand as you knead. You may need to add more flour or water along the way. It takes me about 20-30 minutes to get the dough done.

Preparing the topping
Heat up the oil in the wok and deep fry the *ikan bilis* for half a minute or still till they are crispy.

Rehydrate the mushrooms and dice them.

Add a teaspoon of oil in a wok and brown the garlic. Then add the diced mushrooms and minced pork.

Put in the oyster sauce and dark soy sauce and stir-fry for about 2 minutes. Set aside.

Assembly
Heat up a pot of water till it is rolling and boiling.

Pinch a ball of dough about 2½ cm (1 in) in diameter. Flatten the dough – there is no need to ensure it is of equal thickness – and add to the pot of boiling water. The dough will submerge and will float when it is done, This will take hardly a minute.

If you prefer thin pieces of noodle, put the flattened dough into cold water as this will make it easier to flatten each thinly before you boil it.

Put the cooked noodles into a bowl. Add the broth and the toppings and serve immediately.

HAE MEE
Penang Prawn Noodles

Penang Prawn Mee (Hae Mee in Hokkien) should be somewhere up there amongst the best noodles in the world. The robust, prawny and umami seafood broth, spiced with sambal chilli oil, hits you in the face as you bend to get a spoonful of the soup and noodles.

What makes Penang's version special is the way the flavours of prawns are extracted.

Grey as prawns are to blend into the seabed, their shells carry bright carotenoid pigments which enable them to also blend into colourful backgrounds. Cooking de-natures the shells and frees the carotenoids to reveal their true colors (in more ways than one), which is bright, orange-red. More flavours come from the heads which house the fatty midgut gland, the prawns' organ of digestion. When the heads are blended or crushed, the flavours are released, giving the wonderful colours and special flavours of a well-made Penang Hae Mee broth.

Most cooks will just throw away prawn heads and shells. The amazing thing is that this noodle dish finds it greatness in these discards. So, you can say it is the poor man's noodles. I still have memories of this being sold by the travelling hawker on his motorbike. He advertised his presence with the tok-tok sound from his bamboo clackers while periodically yelling "Hae Mee" in his sharp, shrill voice.

Poor man's noodles it may be, but everyone I know loves it. While there are different ways of making it, depending on one's tradition and whether it is a home or commercial version, my Mum's version is very good.

First, some words about the prawns.

Almost any type of prawn will do but you need enough of them. You want the heads and shells. If you live in an area where small and cheap shrimps are available, use them. Just make sure the prawns you use are fresh. If the heads are dark, that is a sign that they are rotting.

In Singapore these days, wild-caught and small sea prawns are hard to find. Those I usually use are the readily available sea-farmed, medium-sized crystal prawns. This is the kind referred to in the recipe below. A kilogram will have about 50 pieces. I use at least 1 kilo of heads and shells for 10 bowls of broth. As I need only two pieces of prawn meat per bowl, there will be extra meat to freeze for other uses. Thus, making a good prawn noodle is not as expensive as some may think.

Dried shrimp (*ha mai* in Cantonese or *hae bee* in Hokkien) is added to intensify the broth. Some versions will use pork bones and offer pork ribs in the bowl.

This recipe may seem like a lot of work but the preparation work is intuitive and the steps will come naturally. As with all party dishes, effort is needed but your guests will remember your Hae Mee for a long time to come.

Hae Mee

Makes 30 bowls

1 kg (2.2 lb) yellow noodles
1 kg (2.2 lb) rice vermicelli
  (*mai fun, bee hoon*)
3 kg (4.4 lb) prawns
200 g (7 oz) dried shrimps
  (*ha mai, hae bee*)
400 g (14 oz) dried anchovies
  (*ikan bilis*), heads and guts
  removed
10 cm (4 in) ginger, smashed
1 kg (2.2 lb) cubed pork fat to
  make lardon (optional)
30 dried chillies
5 x 5 x 2½ cm (2 x 2 x 1 in) block
  or 4 tbsps shrimp paste
  (*belacan*)
1 kg (2.2 lb) pork ribs
1 tsp salt
200 ml (0.85 cup) lard oil
8 litres (2 gal) water
100 gm (3.5 oz) rock sugar
90 slices fish cake

Topping
60 pieces meat from the prawns
2 kg (4.4 lb) water convolvulous
  (*kangkong*)
2 kg (4.4 lb) bean sprouts
1 kg (2.2 lb) pork loin
10 eggs
Fried shallots

Preparing the prawn stock

Peel and set aside the heads and shells of all the prawns. There is no need to give the prawns a 'hair cut' as everything is used. Set aside 60 pieces of prawn meat for the topping. Keep the remainder for other use.

Heat up 3 tablespoons of oil in a wok and roast the dried shrimps for 10 minutes. Then add the prawn heads/shells and roast till they turn golden orange. Put 8 litres (2 gal) of water in a pot. Add the roasted prawn heads and shells, the dried shrimps, *ikan bilis* and salt. Use a stick blender or standing blender to pulverise them finely. You should see some orange hue in the foam from the fat in the heads. Add the pork ribs, cover and simmer the stock for an hour. Then steep overnight for maximum flavour extraction. You can also do this earlier in the day and let the flavours develop by dinner time.

Sometimes, I will prepare the prawn stock, and the *ikan bilis* and pork bones stock separately and combine them later.

Prepare lardon (see page 237). The lardon can be offered as a garnish but the oil is what you want.

Preparing the chilli paste

To prepare the chilli paste, rehydrate the dried chillies in boiling water for 10 minutes. Cool and blend to a paste. Heat up a cup of oil from the lard in the wok. Simmer the chilli paste in it for 20 minutes. This cooked sambal chilli paste is for flavouring the broth and serving as a dipping sauce with the Hae Mee.

Finishing the stock

Strain the stock. Keep simmering the broth. It is important to taste it as you develop the flavours to learn how each ingredient moves the broth closer to the outcome you want.

While I give the quantities of ingredients in the recipe, the sweetness and saltiness which you prefer may be different from mine. Learn to train your palate to balance the flavours.

Add the rock sugar, *belacan*, and a cup of the prepared sambal chilli paste. *Belacan* will add depth to the seafood flavours. The sambal chilli (with lard oil) will improve the broth, giving it spiciness and mouth-feel. You can also add an additional half a bowl of lard to improve the stock. You need to end up with about 8 liters (2 gals) of broth for 30 bowls.

Don't rush through this broth-flavouring stage. This is where a cook can improve his skills, palate and learn the steps in improving a broth. Sometimes, I ladle out some broth into a bowl and flavour it to find a right estimate of what is needed in the pot.

Preparing the topping ingredients and serving
Use a toothpick or the sharp edge of a knife to de-vein the prawn meat meant for the topping. It is easier to de-vein before you blanch them. Blanch the prawns in the boiling stock using a strainer. Do this in small batches as the prawns need to cook quickly or the meat will fall apart. If you are doing this the day before serving, refrigerate the prawns. They keep well after they are cooked.

Blanch the pork loin in the stock for about 15 minutes.

Slice the boiled prawns into halves. Slice the pork loin and fish cakes. Fried shallot is indispensable. Make your own (see page 238) if you can or buy them.

Rehydrate the rice vermicelli in water for about 20 to 30 minutes, depending on how thick or dry the vermicelli is.

When it is time to serve, assemble a serving of the bean sprouts, yellow noodles, rice vermicelli and *kangkong* in a bowl. Blanch the contents of the bowl in rolling, boiling water for about half a minute. This will also remove the alkaline smell of the yellow noodles. Put the ingredients back into the bowl. Garnish with slices of prawns, pork and fish cake. Pour in the boiling broth and drain. Do it twice.

Add broth to the serving bowl and garnish with fried shallots and serve immediately with plates of sambal chilli paste and lardon on the side.

STOCKS & BROTHS

THE KEY TO A GOOD BOWL of soup noodles is the stock or broth. While making stock can be as simple as dumping stuff in water to simmer, understanding some basics will help you get your stock right. Thus, you will have a good base for tasty noodles, soups or porridge, and flavourful sauces for your stir-fry dishes.

The Chinese have two types of basic stock: superior and normal stock. Better ingredients are used for the former, which may include meat, dried hams, and dried scallops. For home cooks like ourselves, a normal stock using bones will suffice for everyday cooking. I will only prepare superior stock for Chinese New Year dishes.

The most common stock I use is chicken stock. Chicken neck, feet, backbone and wings can be used. This is the reason why I almost always buy whole chickens instead of just going for boneless meat off the shelf. You can get the chicken seller to cut up your chicken or, as I often do, cut it myself.

Unfortunately, not many home cooks will bother to retain the discards for stock making. It will need some organization and storage. So, we rely on commercial stocks or flavourings like chicken powder or demi-glace sauces like oyster or abalone sauce. All these are commercially processed with MSG and other preservative added to prop up the flavours. MSG is used often to mask the lack of freshness and taste in stocks. This makes commercial sense but it is actually a poor way of cooking at home. If you learnt to cook relying on commercial stocks, it can be difficult to wean yourself off.

With better organization, planning and understanding on how to prepare good stock, your meals can improve significantly health- and taste-wise.

In terms of time for maximum flavour extraction, bones will take the longest, followed by meat, prawns and fish. For pork or chicken bones, I will normally simmer for at least two hours. For fish or prawns, an hour will suffice. The use of a pressure cooker will cut down cooking time for stocks by two-thirds. I highly recommend using it and the modern ones are very safe to use.

Bones will give a deep flavour and are great for Laksa or *ramen* broth. Meat will give a sweeter broth that is perfect for Ipoh Hor Fun or other types of rice noodles where you want a more delicate flavour. I will usually fry or roast prawn heads and shells before crushing them to extract the flavours for a stock. For good brown stock (i.e. sauce for steaks), you need to roast the beef bones or meat before making the stock.

Refinement comes in the second stage when you want to reduce, flavour or clarify the stock. As many flavours are oil-soluble, it is advisable to reduce the amount of fat before you make your stock. You do this by trimming your meat. You can, of course, skim the fat off later but that will also remove some of the flavours. Reduced and thickened stock is good for sauces.

You can also make very good vegetarian stock or purees from root vegetables, peas and beans.

Many recipes, especially those for noodles, need a good stock-base. If you follow the noodle recipes and think about what you are doing, you are actually learning to make different kinds of broth, which are also the basis for other types of dishes.

In combination stocks, there are often primary and secondary flavours. I classify below the different kinds of broth.

Ipoh Kai See Hor Fun: Primarily chicken, with secondary seafood flavours. Uses whole chicken with some prawn shells added.

Penang Hokkien Prawn Mee: A seafood broth with secondary flavours from meat bones. Uses more prawn shells, maximizing flavours by roasting and blending. Add some chicken bones for a rounder flavour. Pork bones can be added too. The addition of clams or flower crabs shells also enhance the umami flavours.

Nonya Laksa: Chicken and pork bones with *rempah*. Sometimes prawn shells are added.

Ramen: Pork bones. As these are normally large ones, you need a longer time to extract flavours. Also *dashi*, which is seaweed (*konbu*) and dried fish-flake stock.

Assam Laksa: Seafood broth using fish bones and meat.

Fish Soup Noodles: Seafood broth using fish heads and bones.

Mee Rebus: Potato puree.

Burmese Laksa: Chicken stock with chickpea puree.

ASSAM LAKSA
Penang Laksa

Assam Laksa is a truly Malaysian dish, albeit with Thai influence. It is identified with Penang, the island at the northwest of the Malayan peninsula which has a strong Nonya heritage and a worldwide reputation for superb street food.

Imagine an Indian Mackerel (*kembong*) broth meticulously prepared. Then you add a medley of herbs and spices: Chilli, the complex, fragrant, and fruity torch ginger bud (*bunga kantan*), lots of sour tamarind (*assam*), dried *Garcinia Cambogia* fruit (*assam keping*), blue ginger (*lengkuas*), shallots, laksa leaves (*daun kesom*) and the pungent, heady shrimp paste (*belacan*).

As if that is not flavourful enough, you garnish with umami-laden black prawn paste (*hae kou* in Hokkien), mint leaves, shredded onions, grated pineapple, more *bunga kantan*, and cut red chillies.

Fishy, sour, sweet, fruity, spicy, salty, bitter, minty and umami – this intense recipe has all the works. Assam Laksa is an acquired taste, but, trust me, once acquired, you will be addicted to it. If there is a bowl of noodles which could evoke the strongest cravings, it has to be this.

Ikan kembong is very commonly found in Southeast Asia. It should not be confused with *ikan selar* (Yellowtail Scad) which is larger and broader. You can replace *kembong* with another type mackerel if you need to.

Make sure your fish is fresh. You want to extract all the fishy goodness from meat, bones, skin, heads – everything. If Penang Prawn Mee (page 173) is about maximum extraction of flavours from prawns, Assam Laksa is focused on the fish.

Two types of rice noodles are normally used for Assam Laksa. One is *chou mai fun* or thick rice noodles. The other is *lai fun* which is stickier, smooth and translucent with a springy bite, akin to silver needle noodles (*loh she fun* or *bee tai bak*).

My Mum cooked this dish very often and we got to enjoy a very good, home-cooked version that is far superior to what is available in hawker stalls. My brother, Clement, is very adept at cooking Assam Laksa and it was through him that I was able to get the details of this recipe.

Assam Laksa

MAKES 30 BOWLS

3 kg (6.6 lb) thick rice noodles

Fish broth
3 kg (6.6 lb) Indian mackerel
  (*kembong*)
6 litres (1.5 gal) water

Herbs
5 cm (2 in) blue ginger (galangal,
  lengkuas)
4 stalks lemongrass
4 torch ginger buds (*bunga kantan*)
5 cm (2 in) turmeric root
30 shallots
60 dried chillies

600 g (1.3 lbs) tamarind pulp,
  rendered in 200 ml (⁴⁄₅ cup)
  water, seeds discarded
2 bowls laksa leaves
  (*daun kesom*), stem removed
4 slices dried *Garcinia Cambogia*
  fruit (*assam keping*)
5 x 2½ x 2½ cm (2 x 1 x 1 in)
  shrimp paste *(belacan)*
2 tbsps salt
6 tbsps sugar
400 g (0.9 lb) fresh chilli paste

Toppings
2 cucumbers, julienned
1 small pineapple, julienned
3 large red onions, sliced
1 bunch mint leaves, stems
  removed
2 torch ginger buds, diced finely
10 red chilies, sliced
200-g (7-oz) bottle of prawn paste
  (*heh kou*)

Making the fish broth
Boil the fish in the water for about 5 minutes till the meat is cooked but not falling off the bones.

Next, you de-bone the fish. Pull the meat carefully from the tail end and the whole piece should come off. Then, patiently, remove all remaining bones from the meat. You use a bowl of water to wash the bones off your fingers – the best bone detector and remover, bar none.

Crush as finely as possible the heads and the bones in a mortar or blender. Then add to the broth and simmer for 15 minutes.

Alternatively, add the heads to the broth and using a hand blender, crush the heads. Strain the broth.

It sounds like hard work but it is all done in a jiffy if you have some helping hands.

Flavouring the fish broth
Chop up the herbs, then blend them finely.

Pour all of it into the simmering pot of fish broth, along with the tamarind liquid, laksa leaves, *assam keping*, and shrimp paste.

Use your hands to break the de-boned fish meat into smaller chunks and add them to the broth.

Add the chilli paste. In addition, you can cut some *chilli padi* finely and let each diner decide how spicy he wants his Assam Laksa to be.

Season with the salt and sugar as in the recipe but feel free to adjust further according to your taste.

Preparing the topping

The purpose of the topping is not to make the bowl of noodles prettier but to add other layers of flavours and textures. Serve them in separate bowls and allow the diners to choose what amounts and combinations they prefer.

Assembly

Take enough noodles to half fill a bowl. Blanch them in boiling water for 30 seconds and them put in a bowl.

Scoop in the steaming broth and drain. Scoop in more steaming broth again. This two-step method is to ensure that the noodles are well blanched. Top the noodles and broth with a good portion of the flaked fish from the broth.

Serve immediately, allowing the diners to add toppings of their choice.

RICE

FRIED RICE

Fried Rice is a one-dish wonder that is popular in Cantonese and Southeast Asian cuisine. A wok is best for this. Its ample surface allows for good heat transfer to each rice grain as you stir fry. Although there is a limit to achieving *wok hei* – that desirable smoky, charred fragrance – in the home kitchen, you can make a very good Fried Rice at home by using a wok made from thin iron or steel which transfers heat quickly, and cooking one plate at a time. (See also page 127.)

The second thing about making Fried Rice is to learn to use whatever you have in your fridge or larder. It is a convenient and last-minute option for a meal. Eggs, bottled sauces, dried seafood (*ikan bilis*, dried shrimps) and leftover vegetables can be used. And it makes good use of leftover rice which has dried up in the fridge. Note that soggy and soft rice, even after a day in the fridge, will not make good Fried Rice. If you are cooking rice specially for Fried Rice, use jasmine rice and cook it in a 1:1 rice to water ratio to ensure that the grains, when cooked, would be fluffy and separate.

Learn the basic principles of making good Fried Rice and you can easily vary the ingredients to make Ikan Bilis Fried Rice, Egg Fried Rice, Seafood Fried Rice and so on.

Use the premium brands of soy or fish sauce which have more flavour and are less salty. White pepper and chilies can spice up the dish. Slice the meats thinly or use small chunks of seafood. As for vegetables, even frozen green peas or diced veg can be used. Fresh lettuce, sliced thinly, goes very well with fried rice as a garnish. Scramble the eggs before adding them to the rice. This is to ensure that the eggs do not cause the rice grains to stick together.

MAKES 1 SERVING

1 plate of leftover jasmine rice
2 tbsps oil or lard
1 tsp diced garlic
6 slices lean pork
4 small prawns, peeled
1 tbsp green peas
2 eggs
1 tbsp premium soy sauce
1 tsp fish sauce
½ tsp dark soy sauce
White pepper to taste

Garnish options
Thinly sliced fresh lettuce
Fried shallots

Prepare and put in place all the ingredients as the frying time will be short. Break the eggs into a small bowl. You don't need to beat the eggs.

Heat up the oil in a wok over a small fire till it is hot. Add the garlic, pork, prawns and peas, stir frying briskly to make sure that the garlic does not burn.

After a minute, add the eggs and stir fry for a further minute till it is scrambled and half cooked.

Increase the fire, add the rice, and fry to ensure that the rice does not clump together. Break up clumps with your spatula. You want the rice grains to be separate.

Add the sauces. Sprinkle in some water from time to time to moisten the rice and control the heat.

Sprinkle in white pepper, plate the fried rice and garnish. Serve immediately.

CLAYPOT CHICKEN RICE

I have pleasant memories of eating Claypot Chicken Rice in a coffee shop in my hometown of Petaling Jaya, Malaysia. The scene of claypots being cooked in a line over charcoal fires is mesmerizing. There is an unmistakable smoky claypot scent in the air. You place your order and you wait. And I mean, wait, for 30 minutes or more.

You see it. You smell it. And the wait is always too long. In fact, the wait tells you that it is going to be worth it. The pot finally arrives. The claypot-perfumed rice is steaming hot as you open the cover. You dig your spoon in and take a mouthful. The rice riots in your mouth as the first spoonful is always too hot.

The pieces of chicken are savory and the encapsulated flavours of sweet Chinese sausage (*lap cheong*) and salted fish add bursts of delight in every bite. Then, there is the crunch of spring onions and mustard greens (*choy sum*). The bottom of the pot is scraped to dislodge rice that is burnt to a crust (*fan chiew*). Sometimes, soup is added to soften the flavourful rice crust. It is indeed a meal that is good down to the last morsel.

I had thought that real Claypot Chicken Rice can only be eaten in shops. You cannot replicate the roaring charcoal fire needed to cook this dish in a home kitchen. If you want to eat it at home, you use a rice cooker to make it. So, it is a strange misnomer when home cooks – as my Mum did – call their home-cooked version Claypot Chicken Rice when the claypot is not used! It is a far cry from the real experience but that is the best you can do at home.

True? I was completely mistaken.

You can cook with a claypot over a kitchen stove at home. A claypot is such a great conductor of heat that only a small flame is needed to get some good cooking going.

The best type of claypot to use is the sand claypot (*sa po*). The bottom is not glazed, and it is much cheaper than the beautifully glazed ones. There are some theories about conditioning these claypots but I don't bother as there are contradicting views.

The recipe I share with you is a detailed one which I use when I want to make a very traditional Claypot Chicken Rice. As I cook this regularly, I will sometimes omit and simplify some steps if I do not have certain ingredients. For one thing, my daughters do not like salted fish. However, when I do use salted fish, I use *mui heong ham yue*, a softer variety – with a special fragrance – that breaks up easily when cooked.

This is an easy and intuitive recipe. You will find yourself using it regularly for your everyday dinners at home. As your confidence grows, you will be able to vary the ingredients and try your hand at other claypot recipes.

This recipe aims for smoky rice with a partially burnt crust at the bottom, rice with the right texture – fluffy yet firm and separate, not mushy or sticky, good flavours in the rice, and moist meat that is not overcooked.

Claypot Chicken Rice

Serves 2-3

Half a chicken (about 0.8 -1 kg,
   1.7 - 2.2 lb)
400 g (14 oz) basmati or jasmine
   rice
2 Chinese waxed sausages
   (*lup cheong*), sliced thinly
Salted fish to taste (optional,
   use *mui heong* variety)

Marinade
1 tsp sesame oil
2 tbsps soy sauce
1 tbsp Shaoxing wine (*hua tiao*)
1 tsp sugar
2 tbsps cornflour

Sauce
1 tbsp soy sauce
1 tsp sugar
White pepper to taste

Garnish
1 sprig spring onions, diced
2 red chillies, sliced
1 tsp thick dark soy sauce

Cut off and set aside the backbone, feet and less desirable parts of the chicken for making the stock.

Cut the chicken into small bite-sized pieces, bone-in and skin on. In a bowl, combine the marinade ingredients with the chicken and let it marinate for half an hour. The cornflour will keep the chicken moist and silky in texture when cooked.

Put the pieces of chicken reserved for the stock into a small pot with about 700 ml (3 cups) of boiling water. Leave it to simmer for about an hour. Strain the stock before use.

Put the rice into the claypot. Add an equal amount of stock into the pot. Be careful to keep to the 1:1 rice and liquid ratio.

Cover the pot and cook over a low flame for 10 minutes till the rice is cooked. All the liquid should have been absorbed and the rice is fluffy.

Mix the sauce ingredients in a bowl.

When the rice is cooked, open the lid of the claypot and put in the marinated chicken pieces on the rice. Stick to a single layer to ensure even cooking. Add the sliced sausages on top and include some pieces of salted fish according to your taste. Cover and cook for another 13 minutes. Drizzle in the sauce and cook for another 2 minutes.

At the 25-minute mark, your Claypot Chicken Rice should be done. However, the timing may vary depending on the strength of fire and the type of pot used. Whatever the case, it is easy to see if the meat is cooked.

Serve the pot while it is hot. If dinner starts sometime later, reheat the pot before you serve.

Just before you serve, drizzle on the thick dark sauce, and sprinkle on the diced spring onions and cut red chillies.

Give the rice a good stir to scrape up some of the crusted

rice at the bottom. Accompany with plates of cut chillies in light soy sauce.

To clean the claypot and remove the burnt rice, heat up the pot with some water in it. When the water is hot, use a plastic spatula and gently scrape off the rice.

Quick Claypot Chicken Rice

I have explained at length how to do a really good, traditional Claypot Chicken Rice. However, for a quick dinner, it makes sense to keep things simple. The result will still be delicious.

Use boneless chicken meat which will cook faster. Using a traditional 'sand' claypot, cook the rice just right and you can expect a very good dinner, all done within 30 minutes.

Serves 4

300 g (10.5 oz) boneless chicken
   meat
400 g (14 oz) rice
480 ml (2 cups) water
1 stalk spring onions, diced

Marinade
1 tbsp soy sauce
½ tsp sesame oil
A dash of pepper
1 tsp cornflour
1 tsp dark soy sauce
1 tsp sugar

Put the raw rice into a claypot and cook over a small flame.

Slice the chicken meat into bite-sized pieces. Mix the marinade ingredients and marinate the chicken in it.

After about 10 minutes, lift up the cover of the claypot. You should see that the water has been absorbed by the rice. Put the chicken pieces in one layer on the rice. Pour in any leftover marinade. Close the pot and cook for another 12 minutes till the chicken is nicely cooked.

Garnish with diced spring onions and serve.

STEAMING GLUTINOUS RICE

Glutinous rice is very versatile grain.

It can be served as a main or dessert, sweet or savory. It can be the basis of a simple, homely dish or served as a treasure dish in fine-dining Chinese restaurants. Its sticky quality allows it to be shaped in many ways.

One reason why glutinous rice dishes are not cooked more often at home is, unlike in Thai or Laotian home kitchens, we do not have the right steaming equipment to cook glutinous rice well. The Thais use a rice steamer set which is perfect for steaming sticky rice. The woven bamboo basket, placed on a aluminium steaming pot, keeps the sticky rice from getting too wet when steamed.

Before steaming, the glutinous rice has to be soaked overnight or for at least 3 hours. After about 20 minute upwards of steaming, depending on the quantity of rice, the cooked rice will become translucent.

The Chinese wok set up, even if you line your steamer with cloth, or pot steamer, will not do the job well as the heat and moisture is applied unevenly.

Here is where I find the splatter guard method useful. Use a splatter guard as a base to hold your rice. Put it over a pot or wok (of the same diameter) of gently boiling water. Make sure the guard is high enough so that boiling water does not splash on the rice. Cover the guard to keep the steam in. This simple set up is good for up to 500 g (2.5 cups) of rice – usually sufficient for a household. I usually mix the rice midway to ensure even heating. After it is cooked, the next step is to flavour the rice by steeping or stir frying.

Once you have tried this no-fuss method, you will be encouraged to cook glutinous rice recipes more often.

LOH MAI FUN
Flavourful Steamed Glutinous Rice

Loh Mai Fun, made from glutinous rice, is a breakfast staple which my Mum made regularly for gatherings and parties. Glutinous rice is sometimes used to make desserts (see page 209). .

For this recipe, apart from getting the flavours into the rice, the grains must be separate with a springy, *al dente* bite. Gluey and soft glutinous rice is to be avoided.

The glutinous rice needs to be soaked for four hours or overnight before cooking. It is then drained and fried in a wok and infused with flavour. After that, water is added and the rice steamed in a serving tray.

This dish is great for parties and a ½ kg (1.1 lb) of rice can easily feed 10-15 people. If you prefer, this recipe can be enriched with 'treasure' ingredients like dried scallops or dried oysters. My advice is for you to get confident with cooking good glutinous dishes and master the basics before using more expensive ingredients.

Loh Mai Fun

Serves 10-15

500 g (1.1 lb) glutinous rice
6 dried Chinese mushrooms
2 tbsps dried prawns (*ha mai*)
2 Chinese pork or chicken
    sausages
2 tsps minced garlic
480 ml (2 cups) water
1 tbsp white pepper
1 tsp salt
2 tsps sugar
1 tbsp dark soy sauce
5 tbsps cooking oil

Toppings
200 g (7 oz) peanuts with skins
    left on, toasted
2 stalks spring onions, diced.
4 red chilies, diced
Fried shallots

Soak the rice for 4 hours or overnight. Rehydrate the mushrooms and dice. Rehydrate the dried prawns for 10 minutes and dice. Dice the Chinese sausage.

Heat up the oil in a wok. Add the minced garlic, mushrooms, dried prawns and sausage. Fry for about 5 minutes till fragrant. Drain the rice and add to the wok. Stir fry for 15 minutes, adding a cup of water, white pepper, salt and sugar and dark sauce along the way. Taste and adjust to your liking.

Prepare a wok of water for steaming. Next, move the rice to a tray and pour in another cup of water. Put the tray of rice in the wok, cover, and steam for 40 minutes. At the 20-minute mark, turn the rice with a spoon to ensure that the top layer is cooked properly as well. This needs to be done as steaming does not apply heat evenly, especially when the metal tray conducts heat at the bottom.

Taste the rice and if it is dry or hard because it is undercooked, steam it for another 10 minutes or more till the rice is soft. The steaming process increases humidity and there is no need to add water directly.

When the rice is done, remove from the steamer and let it cool down to room temperature.

Garnish generously with the topping ingredients before serving with chilli sauce.

And yes, always eat this with a pair of chopsticks!

NOTE: If you are using the splatter guard method (see page 190), steam the rice first, then flavour it using a wok.

NASI ULAM
Herb Rice

I have always noticed the Nasi Ulam recipe with its long list of mysterious *daun* in Mum's recipe collection.

Daun means "leaf" or "herb" in Malay, while *nasi* means "rice" and *ulam* means "salad". In the humble kitchens of the Malay kampong, Nasi Ulam uses herbs plucked from the garden or foraged from the nearby forest, and basic dried seafood found in the larder.

Start with fresh herbs. The spicy turmeric leaf and peppery *daun kadok* (wild pepper leaf) will be good to have in your Nasi Ulam, apart from the mandatory basil and mint leaves.

Use a sharp knife to dice the herbs finely. Blending or pounding it won't do as your herbs will become wet and mushy. Cook your rice perfectly, observing the 1:1 water-rice ratio. Jasmine or basmati rice works well for this dish.

My recipe below is best seen as a suggestion. You may not be able to get all the herbs I have listed. Don't fret about it if you can't. Even two to three herbs can make a delicious difference to your rice. Saltiness is important to bring out the flavours of the herbs. This comes from the salt and dried seafood.

Eat Nasi Ulam with some Sambal Belacan and it will be even more *sedap* (delicious). The dish keeps well and tastes even better the day after cooking as the herbal flavours infuse into the rice.

It makes for a great party dish as it is both appealing and appetising on the buffet table and goes very well with other Malay or Nonya dishes like Ayam Goreng Halia (page 35), and Sambal Udang (page 101). Remember to use banana leaves to enhance the plating and party atmosphere.

Nasi Ulam

Serves 6-8

800 g (4 cups) jasmine or
   basmati rice

Fresh herbs
2 tbsps diced mint leaves
1 tbsp diced laksa leaves
   (*daun kesom*)
2 tbsps diced lemon basil leaves
   (*daun kemangi*)
2 tbsps diced turmeric leaf
   (*daun kunyit*)
2 tbsps diced wild pepper leaves
   (*daun kadok*)
2 tsps diced torch ginger bud
   (*bunga kantan*)
6 shallots, sliced thinly

2 tsps seafood flavouring made
   from equal amounts of shrimp
   paste (*belacan*), salted fish and
   dried shrimp.

Seasoning
1 tsp salt or to taste
1 tsp fine sugar

Cook your rice using 1:1 water-rice ratio. When cooked, transfer the rice into a large salad bowl.

Toast the seafood on a dry pan. Then blend or pound into a powder. Set aside.

Dry your herbs before you dice it so that they will not be in clumps. Slice the shallots thinly. Set them all aside.

Add the herbs, shallot slices and dried seafood powder into the rice, adjusting amounts to suit your own taste. Mix gently before adding sugar and adjust the saltiness by adding salt, if needed. This depends on how salty is your seafood powder.

Don't forget to serve it with Sambal Belacan and meat dishes. Nasi Ulam should be enjoyed at room temperature.

For the salted fish, the variety made of Threadfin (*ikan kurau*) is good. As for variations, you can add fresh cucumber cubes for the texture. I sometimes use some diced torch ginger bud for garnishing.

SOME OF THE HERBS WHICH CAN BE USED FOR NASI ULAM.
CLOCKWISE FROM LEFT: TURMERIC LEAF, LAKSA LEAVES (VIENTNAMESE MINT OR *KESOM*), LEMONGRASS (*SERAI*),
TORCH GINGER BUD (*BUNGA KANTAN*), MINT, KAFFIR LIME LEAVES (*DAUN LIMAU PERUT*), THAI BASIL, CALAMANSI,
WILD PEPPER LEAVES (*DAUN KADOK*).

THE ESSENTIAL NASI LEMAK
Coconut Rice

Nasi Lemak is the national dish of Malaysia, the country of my birth. It is, at the core, a reflection of Malay life in a seaside kampong where its essential ingredients can be found on the swaying coconut trees and the fishermen's unsold catch of the day. The coconut rice is at the heart of it, and thus the name, as *nasi* means "rice" and *lemak*, "milky" or "creamy".

Nasi Lemak is quintessential to both Malaysian and Singaporean food culture. Nonya and Chinese cuisines have expanded this dish, adding items like Chicken Curry (page 39), Assam Prawns (page 97), Ayam Goreng (pages 31 and 35) and Beef Rendang (page 87). From a popular *bungkus* – wrapped, takeaway – dish from a street stall, it is now also a rich spread in home parties, hotel buffets and restaurants.

It is a great party dish as diners can pick what they want, children can avoid the spicy items and some adults can choose to go vegetarian. Except for the rice, almost all the items can be served at room temperature.

In this recipe, I want to focus on the essentials of Nasi Lemak. There is no point in having a great Chicken Curry but dreadful mushy rice and an average sambal chili which taste like bottled ones off the shelf. Without the distraction from those big side dishes, the core comes to the fore and that is the kind of Nasi Lemak you want to master.

So, we begin with the *nasi*.

Good Nasi Lemak rice needs the flavour of coconut milk, pandan leaves and salt. If you don't put in enough salt, your rice will taste flat, no matter how *lemak* it is. The rice grains need to be separated, not clumped together. And it needs to have a nice bite to it, not soft and mushy.

The best way of cooking the *nasi* is with a traditional steamer where the rice is cooked by the rising steam of heated water at the bottom. It will ensure that each grain is separated and fluffy.

Use a hybrid two-step method. You cook the rice first in an electric cooker. Keep the ratio of liquid (water and thin coconut milk) to rice at 1:1. When the rice is cooked, transfer it to a steamer. Add in the thick coconut milk and pandan leaves. Stir gently to loosen the rice, then let it steam for another 15 minutes.

If you do not have a suitable steamer, you can still cook the rice well in an electric rice cooker. Add the thin coconut milk into the water (remember to keep the 1:1 liquid-rice ratio). Include the salt and pandan leaves. When the rice has cooked, switch the cooker to 'warm' mode. Add the coconut cream, more pandan leaves and stir gently. Then let it stay in warm mode for another 15 minutes.

For the coconut milk, if you use fresh, grated old coconut, the first press is the thick milk (heavier in cream or fat content) and the second press after water is added gives you the thin milk. You use the thin milk to cook the rice and keep the first press for adding to the rice after it is cooked.

If you can't get hold of fresh thick coconut cream you can use UHT coconut milk. UHT coconut milk comes in different percentages of saturated fat. Choose a coconut milk with low fat content for cooking the rice, and a milk with higher fat content to finish it after cooking. You could also dilute a portion of high-fat coconut milk to make the thin milk for cooking the rice and finish with the undiluted high-fat milk. For example, if you are using a 200 ml (0.8 oz) pack of thick coconut milk, use a quarter of it and add to the water to cook the rice. As long as you observe the 1:1 rice-water ratio, your Nasi Lemak should turn out fine.

Remember that you can also obtain coconut cream by separating the cream that rises to the top of coconut milk. All you need to do is to leave the coconut milk to stand for some time.

Don't go beyond a 1:1 ratio of liquid to rice when cooking the rice. Otherwise, your rice will be too soft and sticky.

As long as you understand these basic principles, you can make any method of cooking rice work for you – even when you use a microwave oven.

Fried *ikan kuning* (Yellowtail Scad) is sometimes called Nasi Lemak Fish. They can be eaten whole when they are deep fried till very crispy. Buy them all cleaned up from the market.

Sliced cucumber is another essential part of Nasi Lemak, though, sometimes, boiled *kangkong* (water convolulus) is served as well.

Nasi Lemak

SERVES 12

1 kg (5 cups) rice
1 coconut, grated
240 ml (1 cup) water
2 tsps salt
10 stalks pandan leaves
300 g (10.5 oz) anchovies
  (*ikan bilis*)
200 g (7 oz) peanuts, skinned
12 eggs

Fried fish
I kg (2.2 lbs) yellowstripe scad
  (*ikan kuning*)
2 tsps salt
1 tsp turmeric powder
1 tsp white pepper
Oil for deep frying

Nasi Lemak Sambal Chilli
See page 230

Squeeze the grated coconut in a cloth to obtain the coconut cream. Set aside. Add 240 ml (1 cup) of water to the grated coconut and squeeze again to obtain thin coconut milk. Set aside. Tie each stalk of pandan leaf into a bundle.

Put the rice into an electric rice cooker. Combine the thin milk and water to make up 1.2 litres (5 cups) and add to the rice. Add salt and 5 bundles of pandan leaves. Start cooking the rice.

When the rice is cooked, add the thick coconut milk and stir gently with a spatula. Taste the rice and add a bit more salt if you find the taste too bland.

Cover the cooker and keep it warm for at least 15 minutes before serving the rice.

Deep fry the anchovies till they are crispy. You can add them to the Sambal Chilli or serve it separately.

You can choose to toast the peanut in the oven or gently fry them in a wok with some oil. The smaller variety of peanuts will cook faster. Note that the peanuts will only be crunchy when they have cooled down.

Put the eggs and enough water to cover them in a pot to hard boil them. Heat up. Once the water is about to boil, switch off the fire and cover the pot for 10 minutes.

A fast way to peel an egg is to do it when it is still warm. Crack the shell all over and peel it under slow, running, cold water. Do not slice the egg when it is still warm if you want the yolk to be smooth; a warm yolk will stick to your knife as you slice.

Marinate the fish for half an hour with salt, turmeric and white pepper. Refridgerate before you fry them. Deep-frying the fish till they are crispy will take between 4-6 minutes depending on the level of fire and size of the fish.

SNACKS & DESSERTS

YAM CAKE

Yam Cake is a savoury breakfast food, dessert or snack which my Mum made very often. Her version was dense and had chunks of yam (taro) in it, adding variation to the texture and taste.

Unfortunately, she did not leave behind her recipe. However, help came from her close friend and companion cook whom we have always known as Har Jie. She had cooked many years with my Mum and through Har Jie, I learned a few more precious recipes, such as this one and the one for Tim Cheong (page 234).

A good Yam Cake starts with good yams which are powdery in texture, and good quality dried shrimps.

Rice flour and wheat starch flour (*tang meen fun*) are added. *Tang meen fun*, which is gluten-free, is normally used for making Har Kau (Shrimp Dumplings) and is translucent when cooked. This flour is also used in Chai Kuih (page 220). You can easily find this flour in supermarkets.

1 kg (2.2 lb) yam (taro)
2 tbsps dried shrimps
1.9 litres (8 cups) water
625 g (5 cups) flour
  or 750 g (5¼ cups) rice flour
5 tbsps wheat starch flour
  (*tang meen fun*)
2 chicken stock cubes
2 tbsps oil
2 tbsps minced garlic
2 tsps salt, or to taste

Garnishing
1 cup fried shallots
1 cup peanuts, roasted and
  crushed
1 cup diced spring onions
3 red chillies, diced

Sauces
Sweet sauce (Tim Cheong),
  see page 234
Fresh chilli sauce, see page 228

Peel the yams and cut them into 1 cm (0.4 in) cubes or slightly smaller.

Rehydrate the dried shrimps and mince them.

Fill a pot with the water. Add the rice flour, wheat starch flour and chicken stock cube and mix.

Heat up a wok with the oil. Add the minced dried shrimps and minced garlic. Fry for about 2 minutes to brown the garlic and roast the dried shrimps.

Add the yam cubes and stir-fry for about 10 minutes, mixing the ingredients well.

Then pour in the prepared stock. Keep stirring with a spatula. The mixture will get starchy and become increasingly harder to stir. Some of the yam will be mashed up while others will stay whole. This is what you want. Taste and adjust saltiness to your taste.

Put the mixture into a steaming tray of about 2 - 3 inches in height. Steam for 90 minutes, then bring it out to cool. After it has reached room temperature, garnish it generously.

Serve with the Tim Cheong and the chilli sauce.

PULUT INTI
Glutinous Rice with Sweet Grated Coconut

Pulut Inti is one of the favourite *kuih*s (Malay cakes) of my childhood. The joy is in the *inti*, toasted grated coconut infused with *gula melaka* (palm sugar). This is placed on top of steamed glutinous rice and wrapped into a flat, pyramid-shaped packet made from banana leaf.

The Nonya version of this cake uses a sprinkling of blue colouring from Butterfly Pea flowers (*bunga telang*). It is flavoursless but it is good to include if you can get it, for, as the old adage goes, we eat with our eyes first.

You need to make sure that the steamed glutinous rice is not mushy. I like to use the splatter guard method as it is convenient (page 190). If you do not have the time to make the packets, you can just make a tray of steamed glutinous rice and place the coconut filling on top of it. It will still be delicious served this way.

MAKES 50

500 g (2.5 cups) glutinous rice
100 ml (0.4 cup) coconut milk
1 coconut, grated
2 tbsps *gula melaka* (palm sugar)
2 tsps brown sugar
½ tsp salt
½ tsp dark soy sauce
3 pandan leaves
6 Butterfly Pea flowers, dried (optional)
Banana leaves for wrapping

Soak the glutinous rice for 2-4 hours.

Steam the rice for 40 minutes or till it is cooked. Remove rice from the steamer and soak it in the coconut milk. The rice will absorb the milk. Soak the dried Butterfly Pea flowers, if using, in 120 ml (½ cup) water to get a deep blue colouring.

To prepare the *inti*, toast the grated coconut in a dry wok. It is important to use grated coconut which have not been pressed. As you toast the coconut, add *gula melaka*, salt and brown sugar to taste. The *inti* needs to be sweet. Add the dark soy sauce to darken the colour. Set aside.

To make the packet, cut the banana leaves into rectangles of about 20 x 15 cm (8 x 6 in). Cut 7 x 5 cm (3 x 2 in) ovals of banana leaves. Place 2 heaped tablespoons of glutinous rice in the middle of a rectangle of banana leaf, shaping the rice into a rectangle. Sprinkle on some blue colouring, if using. Put an oval of banana leaf on the rice and top it with a tablespoon or more of the *inti*.

Fold the long sides of the rectangular banana leaf inward so that the edges form a gap through which the *inti* can be seen. You may have to trim the banana leaf to achieve this. Turn each end of the folded leaf downward to form a packet as shown in the picture. Make packets with the remaining rice and *inti*. Serve.

STEAMING

STEAMING is normally associated with Asian or Chinese cuisine. The tools needed for the process are cheap and easily assembled. For example, the ubiquitous wok in Asian homes can be easily converted to a steamer. This may explain why it is a popular technique in many homes.

The best way to understand steaming is to see it as cooking without direct contact with a strong heat conductor, unlike stir frying in a wok or braising in a pot. Steaming is about cooking in low heat as air is a poor conductor of heat. The Western equivalent is cooking in an oven, which generally uses the same principle but without the inclusion of water. Thus, you can steam a cake and bake a fish!

Through contact with steam, the food is cooked evenly throughout. This is why in steaming, you do not need to turn the food over mid-way to cook its other side.

The science of steaming is simple. Water (liquid) that boils off into a gaseous state (steam) contains high heat energy. This latent heat of vaporization hits the food and cooks it. Steam, by definition, is actually invisible. The 'steam' you see is mist – droplets of water that are suspended in or mixed with air. Of course, when there is steam, you see the mist. But my point is, what you do not see is actually where the heat is and this is what cooks the food. You want to cook the food in the steam which you do not see – under the mist rather than in it.

This explains why wok covers are dome-shaped. The dome holds the mist and ensures that the food is cooked below the mist and not in it. The shape also allows for condensed water droplets to slip back into the water below. For this simple reason, the plate you use to steam the food must be smaller than the circumference of your wok. By experience, you will know that if your plate is too big, it will collect more condensed water.

The exception is the bamboo steamer. Its gaps allow the mist to escape. In fact, bamboo steamers are superior because less water condenses onto the food than when metal covers are used. This is why *pao* (buns) are best steamed using bamboo steamers. Wet buns are disastrous.

Bringing it altogether, steaming has these advantages:

1. Foods which come out best using the slow and low method are suited for steaming.
2. It is harder to overcook the food as the cooking process is gentler.
3. It is suited for odd-shaped food where you want the heat to be evenly applied across its surface (e.g. fish and rice dumplings).
4. It is considered a healthier way of cooking as there is less oil involved.
5. Steaming is similar to using the oven; you don't need to attend to it as it cooks. This is why steaming is very useful when you need to cook various dishes simultaneously.

PRAWN FRITTERS

This dish is perfect on its own as a snack or as a side dish. My Mum made it to accompany her Mee Rebus (page 165). It's irresistibly crunchy, so we often ate it while she prepared the noodle dish.

This is a good recipe to learn. You should be able to imagine the different ways in which you can modify the recipe as you become confident in making this snack.

500 g (1.1 lbs) small shelled
    prawns, diced into 1-cm cubes
750 g (1.6 lbs) plain flour
500 g (1.1 lbs) rice flour
2 tbsps curry powder
1 tsp white pepper
1 tsp five-spice powder
1 bunch of green chives, chopped
1 tbsp salt
1 tbsp sugar
1 litre of water, or more
Oil for deep frying

Mix the diced prawn, the two types of flour, five-spice powders, chives and seasoning together in a large bowl. Add water slowly and mix it into a paste with medium viscosity akin to a pancake mixture. You may need to add more than 1 litre of water depending on the flours used.

Prepare oil in a wok for deep frying. Lower a spatula to just below the surface of the oil. Ladle about 100 ml (0.4 cup) of batter onto the spatula and spread it out into a rough round shape. As the mixture falls onto the spatula, it will begin to bubble and cook. Putting the spatula under the oil as you pour the mixture in ensures that it will not stick to the spatula. The fritter will begin to turn brown after about a minute or so. Cook it till it is crispy. Drain and repeat for the remaining batter.

An alternative method is to use just enough oil so that when you spread the circle of batter on the wok, the cracker is submerged in the oil. Let it sit and cook, ensuring that the underside of the cracker is not burnt due to direct contact with the wok.

CURRY PUFFS

If you are a Malaysian or Singaporean, your mum or grandma must have made some curry puffs that you miss so much. Commercial ones today are not the same. You know that.

My Mum's version has delighted many. The pastry is light, thin and flaky. The filling is delicious: yellow potato cubes, bits of shallots, chicken meat, diced prawns for added umami, all flavoured with chilli, spices and curry leaves. Sometimes, she added wedges of hard-boiled eggs. In fact, the filling is so good that we used to love eating it with white bread too.

Making curry puffs is not for the lazy but keeping the tradition of good home-made curry puff is important. I have made a lot of effort to get the recipe for my Mum's version right. My first try was so disappointing that my wife Jennifer called it "Curry Poofs". After many tries and eventually getting more puffs than poofs, I am glad to taste Mum's curry puffs again.

You can replace the chicken meat with beef, pork, sardine or mutton.

Curry Puffs

MAKES 60

Filling
2 kg (4.4 lb) yellow potatoes
10 eggs, hard boiled and each
  wedged into 8 pieces
500 g (1.1 lb) chicken meat
300 g (10.5 oz) prawn meat,
  diced
4 large white onions, diced
50 g (2 cups) curry leaves
480 ml (2 cups) vegetable oil for
  frying potatoes

Curry paste
20 dried chillies, rehydrated in
  hot water
5 lemongrass bulbs
20 shallots, peeled and diced
5 candlenuts (*buah keras*)
1 tsp turmeric powder
2 tbsps curry powder
2 tsps salt
4 tbsps oil

Inner pastry
500 g (1.1 lb) plain flour
300 g (10.5 oz) margarine

Outer pastry
1 kg (2.2 lb) plain flour
200 g (7 oz) margarine
1 tsp salt
1 tsp baking powder
400 ml (1.5 cups) cold water

Making the filling
My Mum will cut – not mash – the peeled yellow potatoes. They are cut into ½ cm (0.2 in) cubes.

Then the potato cubes are fried in oil for about 10 minutes. This ensures that the potato cubes will not clump up together. Don't overcook the potatoes. Set aside.

Next, make the curry paste or *rempah*. Blend or pound the chillies, lemongrass, shallots, and candlenuts into a paste. Heat the oil in a wok, add the paste, curry powder, turmeric powder, and salt. Slowly cook it over a low flame for about 10 minutes.

Then add the cubed chicken meat, diced prawn meat, diced white onions and curry leaves. Simmer for 5 minutes before mixing in the fried potatoes and stir-fry for another 5 minutes.

Making the pastry
Using the two types of pastry dough and following the rolling method will result in a light, thin and flaky pastry.

To make the inner pastry, mix the flour and margarine and knead into a dough. You will know the dough is done when it does not stick to your hand. Separate into five portions and roll each into a ball.

To make the outer or watery pastry, combine the margarine and flour and add the water in stages as you knead it into a dough. Separate into five portions and roll each into a ball.

Flatten a ball of the outer pastry with a rolling pin. Place a piece of the inner pastry on it, using your fingers to press it to cover the outer pastry. Wrap it with the outer pastry into a ball. Repeat with the remaining balls of pastry.

Leave the balls of pastry to rest for about 1 hour. This will make for easier shaping of the pastry later.

Note that this pastry can be prepared beforehand and kept in the fridge or freezer till needed.

Making the curry puffs

Take a piece of the pastry and flatten it with the rolling pin. Fold once, turn over and flatten it again. Then dab a bit of water on it and slowly roll it like a Swis Roll.

Cut the roll into pieces of about 2½ cm (1 in) wide.

Flatten the cut pieces it into an oval shape. Roll it up by the width and flatten to an oval shape again.

Put a piece of oval pastry on your palm. Spoon about one heaping teaspoon of the filling in the center of the pastry. Add a wedge of hard boiled egg. Fold the pastry over to make a semicircle.

Seal the curved edge of the curry puff. Start at one end of the semicircle, using your thumb and finger to twist the edge to make a crinkle. Continue twisting along the edge till you reach the other end of the semicircle. You should have sealed the curry puff with a rope-like series of crinkles.

Repeat for the remaining pastry and filling. The curry puffs are now ready for deep frying.

You may freeze the curry puffs at this stage if you are preparing ahead. Place the curry puffs on plastic sheets or cling film with a space between each piece. Place in the freezer.

Deep fry immediately after removing the curry puffs from the freezer. Don't thaw. Fry them in batches over low heat. The oil must be gently bubbling. Remove the curry puffs when they are light brown.

Let the curry puffs cool down but they are best eaten when they are warm. If you are serving them later, keep them in a warmer.

CHAI KUIH
Vegetarian Dumpling

Known as Chai Kuih in Malaysia, this vegetable dumpling is often referred to as Soon Kuih in Singapore. However, calling Chai Kuih 'Soon Kuih' is not quite right, as Chai Kuih uses yambean (jicama) for the filling while Soon Kueh uses bamboo shoot.

The best Chai Kuih I have ever eaten was homemade. I can remember vaguely that it was made by Har Jie, my Mum's close friend and cooking companion. I was thrilled to get in touch with her again and, when she visited, she made her Chai Kuih for us and gave me this recipe.

The filling is very tasty and the yambean should be cut by hand to get an irregular, thick and firm strips. Don't use a slicer.

The skin is light and has a nice *al dente* bite. The trick is to use your closed fingers to gently tap and flatten the dough into a round disc before you add the filling and wrap. As the dough is sticky, you will need to coat it with tapioca flour as you flatten it. Although it is not difficult to get the shape of the Chai Kuih right, deft hand work and practice are needed.

Chai Kuih keeps very well. It can be refrigerated or frozen. Steam it briefly before serving.

I will say that you only need to eat it with chilli sauce and avoid adding sweet black sauce.

Chai Kuih

MAKES 25

Filling
600 g (1.3 lb) yambean (jicama,
   bangkwang)
70 g (2.5 oz) carrot
100 g (3.5 oz) skinless belly pork
30 g (1 oz) dried shrimps
5 dried mushrooms
2 tbsp oil
50 g (1.7 oz) minced garlic
2 tsp salt
1 tbsp sugar
1 chicken stock cube
1 tsp dark soy sauce
Pepper to taste
1 cup diced Chinese parsley
1 cup diced spring onions

Skin
140 g (5 oz) wheat starch flour
   (*tang meen fun*)
1 tbsp tapioca flour
350 ml (1.5 cups) water

Making the filling
Peel the yambean and cut into strips of about 2.5 - 3 cm (1 - 1.2 in) in length. Similarly, peel the carrots and cut them into strips. Slice the pork into strips of similar size as well. Rehydrate the dried shrimps. Rehydrate the dried mushrooms too and slice thinly.

Heat up the oil in a wok. Fry the dried shrimps till aromatic, then add in the minced garlic and fry till slightly golden. Put in the pork and stir fry for about a minute. Add the turnip and salt, sugar, stock cube, dark soy sauce and a dash of pepper. Cook it for 30 minutes till soft, turning it over from time to time. Towards the end, add the Chinese parsley and spring onions. Stir to mix well and switch off the fire.

Making the skin
Mix the wheat starch flour and tapioca flour in a bowl and pour in the water. Mix, then gently boil and stir the mixture till you get a sticky and slightly translucent dough. Switch off the fire and let the dough cool.

Shaping the Chai Kuih
Coat both your palms with tapioca flour. Pick up about 25 g (0.7 oz) of dough and roll into a ball of about 2.5 cm (1 in) in diameter. With the ball in one palm, gently tap it with the closed fingers of your other hand to flatten. Transfer the dough to the other hand and continue tapping with your free hand. Alternate from hand to hand. You will need to constantly powder your hands with tapioca flour so that the dough will not stick to them. Flatten till you get a disc of about 12.5 cm (5 in) in diameter.

Put some filling on the round dough, making sure that there is dough all round for wrapping and sealing. Fold the dough over to make a semicircle and seal by pressing the edges together.

Place the Chai Kuih on an oiled tray. Steam them for 7 minutes till the skin turns translucent. Let them cool down, then coat them lightly with oil so that it won't be sticky.

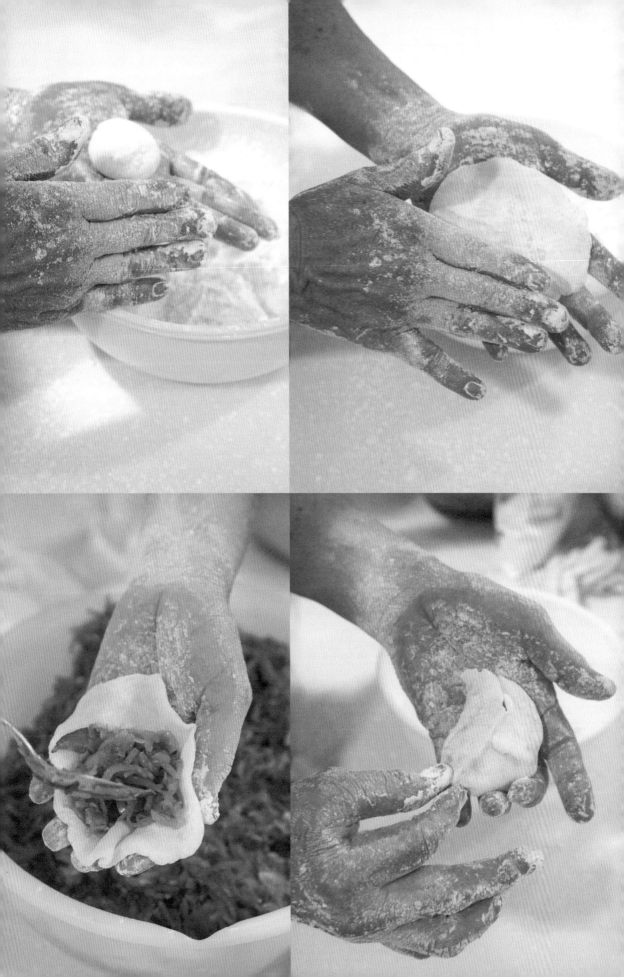

SAGO PUDDING

This is a refreshing, three-ingredient dessert that closes a meal well. It is one of the favourite desserts that my mum-in-law Margaret Loh makes regularly. She will always insist on getting the best variety of *gula melaka*, which is the purer form of palm sugar without any cane sugar added. If you want to push this dessert further up the scale of perfection, you should use freshly squeezed coconut milk. Remember to keep the fresh grated coconut chilled. After you have squeezed out the coconut milk, keep it chilled as well.

Pearl sago (sabudana) is a tapioca staple in some cultures. In Southeast Asia, it is mostly used in desserts and drinks. For this dessert, after the pearls are cooked, some like to pack it in a mould for the sake of presentation.

Everything can be chilled till it is time to serve.

300 g (2 cups) pearl sago
100 g (3.5 oz) *gula melaka*
  (palm sugar)
1 coconut, grated

Heat up a pot of water and when it comes to a rolling boil, add the sago pearls. The outer layer of the pearls will turn from opaque white to translucent. When you can still see a small white dot in the center of each pearl sago, switch off the fire. The sago will still keep cooking. This is to avoid overcooking the pearls. Strain and let it cool, then chill it.

Melt the *gula melaka* gently in a thick-based pot on low fire, stirring constantly with a wooden spatula. Avoid scorching the sugar. A microwave can also be used, which I will recommend as it is more convenient. Use low to medium power. After the *gula melaka* has melted, cool it down and chill.

Add a cup of water to your grated coconut and squeeze it in a cloth. You only need the milk from the first squeeze. Chill the milk immediately.

Assemble the dessert when serving. Put the pearl sago in a glass or bowl. Then pour on the coconut milk and *gula melaka*. You can also place all three ingredients on the table and let your guests help themselves.

LIN CHI KANG
Lotus Seed and Longan Soup

While Chinese cuisine is not well known for its desserts, there are a few which I grew up eating and will miss from time to time.

One of them is the dessert soup called Lin Chee Kang in Cantonese and Cheng Tng in Hokkien. The thing is, we all like the version we grew up with. So, my idea of a good bowl of this is minimalist: I don't like it when it is crowded with all kinds of strange ingredients. To me, Lin Chi Kang has longan, lotus seeds, lily buds, cloud ear fungus, and malva nut (*pang dai ho*i) sweetened by a pandan syrup.

Whether having it hot on a rainy day or as a thirst-quenching cold dessert, a bowl of this finishes off a meal nicely.

Except for the pandan leaves, everything else is dried or dehydrated. So, it is convenient for storage. Get good dried longans which are whole and retain their shape after they have been boiled. The Thai variety is recommended. *Pang dai hoi*, the nut of the *Sterculia lychnophora* tree, becomes jelly-like when soaked in water.

It is best to prepare the sweet, pandan-flavoured syrup separately as the pandan flavour is better retained in the syrup rather than when added straight into the boiling soup. This way, you can also adjust the sweetness easily.

This is not a dessert that you need to boil for long. The flavours of the longans are extracted very quickly. For better control of texture it is best to cook the ingredients seperately and assemble the soup just before serving.

MAKES 20 BOWLS

1 cup dried longans
½ cup lotus seeds
½ cup lily buds
3-5 snow fungus, depending on size
15 malva nuts (*pang dai hoi*)
3 pandan leaves, knotted
300 g (10.5 oz) rock sugar
5 litres (3.5 gals) water

Rehydrate separately the longans, lotus seeds, lily buds, and snow fungus. Remove the bitter green shoot in the lotus seeds, if any. Soak the malva nuts in warm water till they expand and remove the skin and seeds with your fingers. Cut the snow fungus into bite-sized florets.

To prepare the syrup, slowly boil the rock sugar in 480 ml (2 cups) water. When the sugar has melted, switch off the fire, and add the pandan leaves.et it steep.

Bring 5 litres (3.5 gal) of water to a simmer and cook the lotus seeds and lily buds in it for 20 minutes. Add the cloud ear fungus and the dried longans. After 5 minutes, the dessert is ready.

Serve in a bowl with the malva nut "jelly" and syrup according to taste. You can, of course, add other ingredients like sago, dried persimmon, and orange peel.

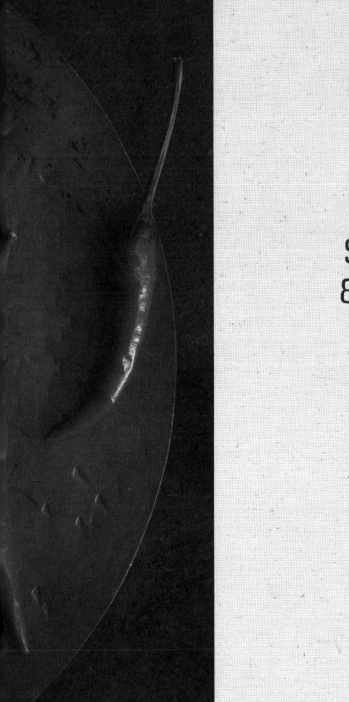

SAMBALS
& SAUCES

FRESH CHILLI SAUCE

This sauce is good for Hakka Yong Tau Foo (page 143), Yam Cake (page 207), Chee Cheong Fun and Fried Rice Vermicelli (page 155). It can also be used as a dipping sauce for Si Yau Kai (page 27). It can be kept in the fridge and used in other ways. As large red chillies are not spicy enough, I normally add some bird's eye chillies.

30 large red chillies
10 bird's eye chillies (*chilli padi*)
1 tbsp white vinegar
2 tbsps water
1 tsp sugar

Blend or pound the chillies.

In a small pot, heat up the chilli paste along with the rest of the ingredients for about 5 minutes.

BASIC CHILLI PASTE

This sauce can be use for the Penang Prawn Noodles (page 173)

30 dried chillies
240 ml (1 cup) oil
1 tbsp water
1 tsp salt

Rehydrate the dried chillies. Cool, then blend to a paste.

In a wok or pot, heat up the oil. Add the chilli paste, and salt and simmer for 20 minutes. Slowly add water to achieve the thickness you prefer.

After 15 minutes, it is done. Cool and store in a jar.

BASIC CHILLI SAMBAL

125 ml (½ cup) lard
100 dried chillies, rehydrated
5 x 5 x 2½ cm (2 x 2 x 1 in) block
   or 4 tbsps shrimp paste
   (*belacan*)

Toast the shrimp paste till fragrant.

Blend the rehydrated dried chillies into a paste.

Heat the lard over low fire, add the toasted shrimp paste and the chilli paste. Mix well and simmer for 15 minutes.

SAMBAL BELACAN
Shrimp Paste Sambal

A simple plate of white rice, Sambal Belacan and fresh cucumber has kept many generations of Malay families happy.

If there are days when your dishes are not "happening", a good Sambal Belacan can save the day. It is a super flavour enhancer. When you couple umami-ladened *belacan* (shrimp paste) and fiery chillies, you have a combination that satisfies a few cravings at one go.

You need *belacan* of course. You need to toast it to mellow the fishy flavours and add a smoky dimension to what is already a complex ingredient. Use the wet type which comes in blocks. The powder or freeze-dried blocks won't do as the taste is not as intense.

Fresh red chillies these days are not as spicy as they used to be; it depends on the season or where you get yours from. You can add some fiery *chilli padi* (bird's eye chillies). My preference is to avoid over-spicing it so that diners can eat more of it. That said, if your family are seasoned chilli eaters, ignore my advice.

Shallots will add some sweetness and body. My mum's version includes some turmeric and blue ginger (*lengkuas*) too.

Sambal Belacan is one reason why the *lesong* (mortar and pestle) is still in my kitchen. Texture is important to Sambal Belacan and when you pound it, you will get flaky chilli pieces and flavours that meld better together. It is best eaten fresh, right after you make it. With the *lesong*, it is easy to make small quantities when you need it. To avoid tearing your eyes, wear a pair of swimming goggles!

If you are making a large quantity, the result is not tragic if you have to use the electric blender. Remember to add some sugar.

5 fresh red chillies
5 shallots
2 cm (0.8 in) blue ginger
  (*lengkuas*, galangal), skinned
1 cm (0.4 in) turmeric (*kunyit*),
  skinned
1 tsp shrimp paste (*belacan*),
  toasted
1 tsp sugar
Limes
Kaffair lime leaves (d*aun limau
  perut*), chopped

Pound the chillies, shallots, root spices, shrimp paste and sugar. Add the ingredients in stages for easier pounding.

Squeeze in some lime juice for the flavour and to add some liquid. Sprinkle on some chopped kaffir lime leaves just before serving.

NASI LEMAK SAMBAL
Sambal for Coconut Rice

Without sambal, there is no Nasi Lemak. And without a good one, your Nasi Lemak won't be great either.

This sambal, unlike Sambal Belacan is not a dipping sauce. As it is to be eaten with rice in more generous portions, it should not be as chilli-intense as other sambal varieties. Add more shallots and onions, and moderate the spiciness by using dried chillies. It should also be sweeter, providing a contrast to the savoury coconut rice. Good Nasi Lemak Sambal Chilli should be sweet with a tinge of salty and sour undertone.

The recipe given is an ultimate version which you can easily simplify. I have made a version with just chilli paste, shallots, oil, salt and sugar. If you are serving Nasi Lemak with extras like curries, Sayur Lodeh or Assam Prawns (page 97), simplify the flavours of your sambal.

60 dried chillies, rehydrated and de-seeded
20 shallots
240 ml (1 cup) oil
2 large onions, sliced
4 tsps *gula melaka* (palm sugar)
3 tsps sugar
2 tsps salt
2 tsps tamarind paste

I use the wrinkled, long variety of dried chilli which is less spicy than the smoother, shorter ones. Soak the dried chillies in hot water. When soft, snip into two and de-seed with a small spoon or the tip of the scissors. Be kind to your fingers. Blend the chillies finely. Set aside.

Blend the shallots coarsely. Set aside.

Heat up the oil in the wok. I normally use the leftover oil from frying the *ikan bilis* for the Nasi Lemak. Add the shallot paste and sweat it over low flame for 10 minutes. This releases the sugar in the onions and also removes their sulphuric fumes.

Then add the chilli paste and simmer for about 15 minutes. Towards the end, add the slices of large onions and switch off the fire.

A variation of this recipe includes fried *ikan bilis*. If you are doing this, fry the ikan bilis first and set aside. Add the fried *ikan bilis* after the sambal is done. Remember that ikan bills will add saltiness to your sambal chilli so taste and add salt only if required. The ikan bilis will not be crispy as they would have absorbed the chilli, and the taste gets better with time as the flavours come together.

Both sambals are to be served at room temperature. They can be put in jars and stored in the fridge.

SAMBAL BELADO

The is an Indonesian chiili paste which is coarsely pounded or blended. It goes very well with Ayam Goreng (page 31), Nasi Ulam (page 197), fried fsh and Fried Brinjal (page 140). Sufficient oil is needed for the correct mouth-feel. I prefer to keep the bright red of the chillies and, for this reason, I caramelise the onion and tomato paste before adding the chilli paste.

20 large chillies
10 bird's eye chillies (*chilli padi*)
2 large red onions
1 large tomato
2½ cm (1 in) blue ginger
   (galangal, *lengkuas*)
240 ml (1 cup) water
1 tsp salt
1 tbsp sugar
2 kaffir lime leaves (*daun llmau
   perut*)
480 ml (2 cups) oil

Blend or pound the chillies coarsely. Set aside.

Dice the red onions, then blend or pound them with the tomato coarsely. Set aside.

Dice the kaffir lime leaves and blue ginger.

Heat up the oil in a wok. Add the onion and tomato paste and the diced ginger and simmer for about 15 minutes.

Add the chilli paste, water and salt. Simmer for another 5 minutes. Adjust to your taste by adding salt or sugar.

Towards the end, add the diced kaffir lime leaves.

THE SECRET IS IN THE SAMBAL

SAMBAL IS VERY POPULAR in Southeast Asian cuisine, especially amongst the Malays and Nonyas. I grew up eating all kinds of sambals and my Mum ensured that I started early on this fiery addiction.

If you are wondering where the distinctive taste of any good Malay stall or Nonya restaurant comes from, in all likelihood, it has to do with sambal.

Sambal is basically made from chillies along with various condiments – like shallots, *belacan* (shrimp paste) and lemongrass – depending on the type of sambal one is making. When the raw ingredients are mixed into a paste, it is sometimes called *rempah*.

Some sambals are eaten raw, like Sambal Belacan. Most are gently cooked in a wok with some oil added. As the flavours of most herbs are oil-soluble, the tastes will fuse, resulting in a sambal with mellowness and a wonderful mouth-feel from the oil and caramelized onion-based paste.

Different chillies can be used, fresh or dried (which needs to be rehydrated), and they all give slightly different results. The smaller and fiery *chilli padi* are often added to notch up the spiciness. Use the best chilies you can find in regards to flavour, texture and spiciness.

The traditional way of pounding and bruising chillies in a mortar and pestle (*lesong*) is still the best way of releasing and mixing the ingredients. The process will bring tears to your eyes but you will smell the flavours developing as you add various ingredients. Pounding, as opposed to grinding in an electric blender, produces a noticable different flaky texture. However, an electric blender will work too, especially when you want speed and convenience when making a huge lot.

I should add that using the *lesong* has its own convenience too, especially when you want to quickly pound a small amount of herbs. I find it indispensable in my kitchen.

As for cooked sambal, the key is to caramelize or sweat the onions patiently in an amount of oil which is roughly equivalent to that of the onions.

Almost always, these appetizing sambal dishes are enjoyed with white rice and eaten traditionally using your fingers.

TIM CHEONG
Sweet Sauce

Tim Cheong is commonly used in Malaysian cuisine for dishes like Chee Cheong Fun, Hakka Yong Tau Foo (page 143), Yam Cake (page 207), and Penang Rojak (page 138). You will find that in terms of flavour and texture, this Tim Cheong is much better than commercial ones.

2 tbsps oil
2 tbsps flour
2 tbsps brown soy bean sauce
  (*tau cheong*)
3 tbsps sugar
½ tsp dark soy sauce
240 ml (1 cup) water

Heat up the oil in a wok. Add the flour and stir over low heat till you get a smooth paste. You are using an equal amount of flour and oil to make a smooth *roux*. The stirring can go on for more than 15 minutes till you get the paste smooth and fragrant.

Now add the *tau cheong*, dark soy sauce, and sugar. Add the water gradually and keep stirring. Taste and adjust the sweetness and viscosity of the sauce. This can be achieved by adding water, the length of time you cook the sauce and how vigorously you stir it. How thick and sweet the sauce needs to be depends on what you are eating it with, and to your preference.

GINGER SAUCE

5 tbsps diced old ginger
3 tbsps diced young ginger
3 tbsps diced garlic
3 tbsps sesame oil
3 tbsps cooking oil
2 tbsps oyster sauce
2 tbsps soy sauce
1 tbsp sugar

Blend or pound the old ginger. Squeeze out juice from the diced young ginger. Reserve the ginger. Dice the garlic.

Combine the sesame oil and cooking oil and heat in a wok over a small flame. Add the garlic and, when it has browned, add the ginger pastes. Simmer for 10 minutes, stirring periodically to ensure that the paste is not burned.

Add the oyster sauce, soy sauce, and sugar and simmer for another 10 minutes. Adjust the taste to your liking by adding soy sauce or sugar.

KERISIK
Toasted Coconut and Coconut Paste

1 fresh coconut, grated

In a wok on low fire, toast the grated coconut till it is golden brown, but not burnt. Stir constantly to prevent burning. It will take about 30 minutes.

To make the coconut paste, use a mortar and pestle to pound the toasted coconut in small batches to obtain an oily and sticky paste.

If you squeezed the grated coconut to extract the milk, it will be harder to produce an oily Kerisik. So, leave the milk in. One grated coconut can produce a bowl of Kerisik. Store the bulk in the freezer for future use.

LARDON

Lardon can be offered as a garnish. Its flavour and mouth-feel in a broth is fantastic. Lardon can be prepared beforehand and stored in the fridge for weeks.

1 kg (2.2 lb) pork fat

Cut the pork fat into 1 cm (0.4 in) cubes.

In a pan, slowly heat up the cubed fat. The oil will slowly flow out and fry the rest of the fat. Keep the fire low so as not to burn the lardon. It will take about an hour to do it right.

When the cubes have shrunk to a quarter of their original size, increase the fire to get the lardon nicely browned.

FRIED SHALLOTS

Fried shallots are essential to many of the recipes in this book.

We are talking about shallots here and so the less fragrant round, small onions won't do. Shallots have a sharp end and they are generally deeper purple in colour. The layers of flesh are also thinner and dryer, making it easier to crisp them up.

Peeling them is less a tearful experience if you wear a pair swimming goggles or soak the shallots in water as you peel. If you have a food processor with a chopper, slicing them will be a breeze.

Fried shallots keep well in a jar in the fridge and it makes sense to make and keep a large batch.

Shallots, peeled and sliced

Heat up some oil in the wok over medium flame and, when the oil sizzles and bubbles, add the sliced shallots in, a small batch at a time.

When they have turned golden brown, remove and drain. They should be crispy after they cool down to room temperature.

FEASTING WELL IN LIFE

THERE IS A NEW FASCINATION with food in our globalized world today. We have terms like "gastronomic tourism" and "food porn" while chefs are international celebrities.

I am all for creativity and innovation. However, we would do well not to neglect the traditional aspects of food, which bring depth and beauty to the human experience, making it less selfish, less self-aggrandising, where meals are set in the classical context of giving, community, family and relationships.

The Bible offers some of these helpful perspectives.

Hosting a guest at one's dinner table can serve as an expression of welcome and acceptance. To eat with someone is to embrace him. Jesus often ate with the rejects and outcasts of society, an association that drew the criticism of the self-righteous religious elite of His day. He dined with tax collectors and prostitutes, sharing food with them and engaging them in conversation. How often do we find ourselves connecting with others, even strangers, over a shared meal?

Meals and feasting also carry the idea of resting from labour. The Bible takes this further in its portrayal of a heavenly banquet as "salvation rest" from work, and the ravages of sin and suffering in this world. When we feast and eat, we naturally experience an inner sense of rest. One of the most well-known passages in the Bible must be Psalm 23. The psalm begins with the image of a guiding Shepherd but ends with us being served by a Chef – "You prepare a table before me...." (Psalm 23:5). Each meal can be a picture of that rest, even if it just provides a brief respite in the midst of the stress of everyday life. Take time to enjoy food. If you are eating with someone, enjoy the conversation and company while being fully present and engaged.

Associated with the idea of rest is also the theme of re-gathering. This is one reason the Bible refers to meals when it describes homecoming events such as the Parable of the Banquet (Luke 14:15-24). With each meal, whether in our homes, especially the Chinese New Year reunion dinner, or in church at the Lord's Supper, we anticipate the great gathering in heaven with Christ.

The idea of welcome, rest and home is also powerfully portrayed in the Parable of the Prodigal Son (Luke 15:11-31). The younger son squanders away his inheritance. He returns in shame, hoping for his father's forgiveness yet feeling unworthy to be called his son. His father does much more than forgive. He throws a lavish feast which includes a fattened calf to celebrate the restoration of a son who had gone astray. He exclaims: "Let's have a feast and celebrate. For this son of mine was dead and is alive again; he was lost and is found." To gather around the table again reflects the reinstatement of the son's position in the family. In feasting, the family celebrates the ties that bind. Yes, a family that eats together stays together.

In fact, the Church eats together as it gathers to partake in Holy Communion or the Lord's Supper. Christians are simply doing what they were commanded to do by Jesus. In doing so, they experience once again welcome and acceptance into God's family, the rest He provides from the toils and troubles of life and celebrate His goodness. Christians are simply grateful that they are forgiven and accepted by God the Father, and they remember this over a spiritual meal.

I look forward to seeing my mother who is now with the Lord at the Heavenly Banquet. That will be a double homecoming for me.

I hope this cookbook will not only inspire you in your cooking but in your reflection on the meaning of life, family and community. I believe that our experience of food and cooking can be made richer and more meaningful when it is experienced as designed by our Creator.

I recall the promise in the words of Jesus, "I have come that they may have life, and have it to the full." (John 10:10).

My prayer for you is to have this life to the full, where food and feasting is experienced in the context of rich relationship with your friends, family and your Creator.

Jesus also said: "'Behold, I stand at the door and knock; if anyone hears My voice and opens the door, I will come in to him and will dine with him, and he with Me." (Rev 3:20).

He is offering "food" that is deeply satisfying and I pray that you may know and experience this.

TONIGHT'S MENU:

HOME STYLE NASI LEMAK

(STEAMED)
"KUKUS"
RICE   SERVED   WITH:
AYAM GORENG · MIXED VEG
ASSAM PRAWNS · LOTS OF LOVE

INDEX

Pages with recipes are set in bold.

ACKNOWLEDGEMENTS

To my dearest wife Jennifer for embracing my Mum so warmly and for your
faithful love and support in everything that the Lord has entrusted me with.

To my two beautiful girls, Sarah and Deborah, who always show appreciation
when I cook and who remind me constantly not to be a food snob.

To my Mama, who always helps to keep my home clean and neat whenever she visits,
for her love all these years for all in the Wong family which made the
presence of two mothers in a family a point of blessing rather than tension.

To my brother Clement who gave input for a few recipes here, and my sis-in-law Mary
for her patient caregiving when my Mum was very ill.

To my parents-in-law Tee Fun and Margaret for their love, generosity and encouragement,
especially by giving me feedback that I may improve when I tried to continue
my Mum's cooking legacy. Your love for Mum has also reflected God's love for her.

To my wife's brother, sister and their families, and my nephew and nieces of the Wong family,
for patiently sampling my cooking and the many dishes that were works in progress.

To Lucy Kwok, my personal assistant for many years in St James' Church, for her personal
friendship to me, Jennifer and my Mum. And along with Fe her helper,
and all in the Food Ministry at St James' Church, for the years of support and cooking fellowship.

To all the ladies of St Andrew's Cathedral who have so quickly risen up to the challenges
and embraced the joys of community cooking.

To Nita, my parents-in-law's diligent helper – an eager learner who is becoming a budding cook herself.

To Har Jie for being a faithful family friend and companion cook to my Mum
and being willing to share whatever recipes she knew with me.

To Dr Leslie Tay and other food enthusiasts who have supported my blog and
inspired me with their passion for our food culture.

To the Bishop of the Diocese of Singapore (Anglican), Rennis Ponniah,
for his faithful support, not just in ministry work, but also in life.

And most of all, to our loving God and Father for the gift of salvation through His Son, Jesus Christ,
that has so wonderfully transformed my life and that of my family, not least my mother.

About the Author

Terry Wong is the author of the popular cooking blog, The Food Canon, which shares the legacy of recipes he inherited from his late mother.

Terry grew up in Petaling Jaya, West Malaysia, before moving to Singapore in 1983 to study, work and settle down. The blog has inspired many home cooks and seeks to keep Malaysian and Singaporean food traditions alive. He also actively encourages communal and home cooking to restore family and community culinary traditions eroded by modern life.

He works as an Anglican clergyman and is married to Jennifer. They have two daughters, Sarah and Deborah.